BART CONNER

WINNING THE GOLD

BART

CONNER

WINNING THE GOLD

with Coach PAUL ZIERT

WARNER BOOKS

A Warner Communications Company

Printed in the United States of America
First Printing: May 1985
10 9 8 7 6 5 4 3 2 1

Cover photographs by Daniel Wagner

Library of Congress Cataloging in Publication Data

Conner, Bart.
   Bart Conner : winning the gold.

   1. Conner, Bart.   2. Gymnasts—United States—
Biography.   3. Olympic Games (23rd: 1984 : Los Angeles,
Calif.)   I. Ziert, Paul.   II. Title.
GV460.2.C66A34   1985   796.4'1'0924 [B]   84-40655
ISBN 0-446-51333-4

Designed by Giorgetta Bell McRee

To my coach, Paul Ziert, who said to me,
"There's nothing wrong with chasing dreams,
you just might catch one."

I caught one.

Thanks to Paul Ziert, I had a story worth telling. And thanks to Linda Perigo Moore, who understood my passion and was willing to cartwheel back and forth across the country to help me put this story on paper.

Each day I thank God for my parents, Harold and Jackie, and brothers, Bruce and Michael, for their belief in me.

Thanks to Gram and Pap. Pap died one year before the Olympics, but his sparkling eyes always reminded me that the world was a pretty wonderful place.

And thanks to Les Lange for lifting me up to my first set of parallel bars, and John and Kathy Burkel for seeing and outlining a future for me.

To Dr. Lonnie Paulos, Keith Kleven, and Keith's assistant, Susie Heins, for guiding me through the most progressive rehabilitation program in the world.

Thanks to my friends Andy Olson, the Caesars Palace family, and Sunworld International Airways for supporting my rehab efforts this year.

And to my friend Irene at the Kettle restaurant in Norman, Oklahoma, for fixing me those banana split cakes for good luck!

CONTENTS

INTRODUCTION

During the most fantastic week of my life I had the honor of winning two Olympic gold medals: one in the gymnastics team competition and a second on the parallel bars. But I was lucky to have been there at all. Eight months before the Twenty-Third Olympiad, my chances of even making the team seemed pretty remote.

It was December 4, 1983. Nagoya, Japan. The Chunichi Cup. Three million TV viewers were watching international teams jockey in an emotional lineup for Los Angeles. Ours is a sport scored by emotion. It's not like a race—where if you run the fastest, you win. At this level of competition everyone there was capable of doing a perfect routine. We could all cross dead even over an imaginary finish line. The winning, then, rested in the *minds* and *opinions* of the judges. Subjective judgments are always a composite of past events: How does a guy usually perform this routine? What improvements has he made? What tiny flaw or wobble might be overlooked this time? Anybody who would be an Olympic judge was watching at that moment. And judging for L.A.

My coach lifted me to the rings and the crowd became attentive. I pulled up into my first move, a *dislocate* through an *inverted cross*. It's like an upside down *iron cross*—with my arms spreading the rings apart and my feet sticking straight up in the air. All I could see were the olive drab mats of the Japanese team—the ugliest mats in the world. Blood filled my head and I could feel the ridges on the wooden rings at my fingertips.

It was a good swing. Comfortable. On the mark.

Sounds were faint and far away—a cough in a corner of the arena, the rustling of somebody's plastic raincoat, fluorescent lights buzzing overhead.

Suddenly, right next to my ear, I heard that sound. A fast, loud rip, like when you yank apart pieces of Velcro. The pain was hot and sharp.

My left bicep had ripped off the bone and snapped down my arm like a window shade.

Upside down in Japan, the first word to cross my mind was, *Damn!* I *kipped* into an *"L" position* and contemplated my next move—a press to a *handstand*. The *"L"* had to be held for two seconds, and after that time I had made my decision. I opened my grip, dropped eight feet to the mat, and told myself, "You've still got seven months to fix this thing before the Olympic trials."

Lots of other people were saying other things:

"He's too old, anyway."

"Now he's hurt."

"There's no way ol' Bart can make it back this time."

They were wrong.

Lucky? Forget it. Luck is when things happen *to you*. Bart Conner *makes* things happen.

Three times he was a member of the U.S. Olympic Gymnastics Team. Fourteen times he was an NCAA All-American. He was a finalist in thirteen World Championships—that's a U.S. record. He won the American Cup three times—that's also a U.S. record. He's the *only* American gymnast, male or female, to have won gold medals at every level of gymnastics competition both national and international.

And none of this came without grief. In 1980 he and the rest of America's Olympians were victims of a futile political gesture that forced them to walk away from years of preparation. While competing for Oklahoma University, Bart was also representing this country as a World Champion. He was so far above his collegiate peers that when his team traveled to another campus, rival fans tried to break his concentration. Finally, in 1983, at the gymnastically ripe age of 25, he suffered an injury that would have crippled most of us.

How he survived—the myriad mental, physical, and emotional factors that brought him to success in Los Angeles—that's not a *good luck* story. But it is *quite* a story. And whether we're coaches guiding potential Olympians, parents helping youngsters explore any sport, or simply people trying to overcome outrageous and unjust obstacles, we can all learn from it.

How did he do it? Is he just a physically superior human being? A *natural-born* athlete? I'm asked these questions every day. And yet most people are shocked when I tell them that Bart Conner is by no means the most physically talented young athlete I've ever coached. Nevertheless, he may certainly be the most determined.

It's easy to play amateur psychologist when you see determination like Bart's. You can look at the level of his skills, at his accomplishments, the pain, the years of work and sacrifice, and you can come away with a quick verdict: the guy's compulsive. And compulsion—particularly in a young athlete—scares people. I've coached kids at every skill level, and many parents have said to me, "I'd never let my child become so compulsive about gymnastics. All those hours in the gym. It's unhealthy."

What many fail to recognize is that Bart's *compulsion* is for life—not sport. Gymnastics is merely the method he chooses to express a positive and determined joy of accomplishment. Had he chosen to do so, he could have applied to any field the same mental discipline and the same problem-solving skills that won him two Olympic gold medals. The techniques of discipline—the mechanics of problem-solving, the joy of accomplishing at our own best levels—that's what the rest of us can learn from him.

CHAPTER 1

Headstands Against the Wall
—The Early Years

I started gymnastics when I was ten years old. Something that I've never forgotten is that my mom and dad started right along with me—driving me to practice, sitting in the lobby of the Y.M.C.A. while my classes were in session, going to meets, sweating through every move and every fall in every competition.

My parents have continuously given this kind of support to me and my two brothers. And it wasn't easy. Besides running me to the gym, my mom took us to soccer, speed skating, baseball, swimming, diving . . . You name it and we were on the move. On countless dark winter mornings the four of us would pull into our driveway just as the neighbors were turning on lights and making coffee. But we had been up for hours and were coming back from skating practice. Later, while I was competing in gymnastics, my brothers, Bruce and Michael, were nationally ranked speed skaters. My parents encouraged us to participate in sports, but they never dictated which ones or to what degree. We were always told, "You must decide. If you want to go to the game, we will take you. If you don't want to go, we'll stay at home." All they asked was that the motivation come from us. Oddly enough the three of us ended up in sports that were somewhat unusual. Fifteen years ago everybody else played baseball, football, and basketball—and we did those things too—but nobody was into speed skating and gymnastics. In the beginning I stuck with gymnastics mainly because it was easy for me. I was small, I had a good deal of upper-body strength, and in this sport, those are real advantages.

I was also attracted to gymnastics because of what you might call a weird habit: I liked to stand on my head. My mom says that even as a toddler I used to lean over the edge of the sofa and hang upside down for as long as an hour. She really had to keep an eye on me when I was outside. Our house had huge windows that overlooked a city park. I remember Mom standing at those windows while my brothers and I sailed off the swing sets or flip-flopped off the merry-go-round. I'd always be the one who was swinging from the basketball backboard or climbing on the roof of the parkhouse and jumping off into the bushes. We even invented a game in which we would jump on a swing set, swing as high as possible, and then—as the forward arc of the swing reached its full height—fall out into a backward flip. Our parents still tell people about our "record summer"—thirty-seven stitches among the three of us.

The park was the real focus of our lives then. We played baseball in the summer and we skated in the winter. When the Chicago snow got deep, the parks department would plow the ice rink and create a mountainlike perimeter of snow. I used to skate full blast to the edge of the rink, and as soon as my feet left the ice, I'd flip over and land square in the middle of the snowbank.

Anybody can do that stuff in a pile of leaves, but snowbanks are a real challenge.

Like most siblings, my brothers and I fought constantly. Our family room was covered with shag carpeting and many times my knees and elbows were covered with the blisters I got from wrestling on that floor. Things were usually pretty wild, as illustrated by our games of "Higher than the Ground." It was a variation of Tag with two major differences: you had to stay higher than the ground, and our beagle, Tippy, was "it." The perfect spot to play was in the basement, with good "climbable" objects like the workbench, the washer and dryer, or the stairs. First we'd bring out long sweat socks, pull them halfway on our feet, and get up on something higher than the ground. Then we'd dangle the socks at Tippy and he'd freak out. We'd jump up onto the washer or a file cabinet and the dog would jump right along with us because he wanted to get those socks. If he caught you, he might cause you to fall and then, of course, you'd lose the game.

I'm not suggesting this is how you should get into gymnastics, but when we got tired of Higher than the Ground, we'd take all of our sheets, blankets, and pillows and pile them in the corner of the living room. Then we would take a running start down the hall stairs, round the corner, flip off the sofa, and land in the pile. The first time my mom saw that one, she signed us all up for an acrobatics class. After the first lesson, I informed her that I would never return because we were the only boys in a room full of girls!

My parents were wonderful because they were willing to let us be so physically active. Doing flips in the living room and standing on the washer seemed like perfectly normal activities for us because we knew that objects in our house were meant to be used and enjoyed. It was always as much "the kids' house" as it was "the adults' house." Needless to say, there were only a few safe places for Lladro porcelain or Steuben crystal in our house.

When I got a little older, I taught myself to do simple flips and headstands. I was particularly fond of annoying my mother by standing on my head whenever she was quizzing me about school.

As soon as I'd hit the house, I'd throw down my books, flip upside down, and wait for her to say something about how all she ever saw was my feet.

One day she really got the last laugh. I came in, pulled my usual stunt, and she whipped upside down right alongside of me! It was a pretty weak headstand (she had to lean her feet against the wall), but it may have been the first time that I recognized how far she was willing to go to respect and even experience the things that interested me. I know now that this focus upon everything that my brothers and I did was what made us all so self-confident. I once heard her tell someone that kids were only around for fifteen or twenty years and that during that time they deserved their parents' undivided attention.

I probably kept her attention, all right. I never walked if I could have run, I never sat still if I could have moved, and if left alone with any large object, I could have found a way to climb it and jump off. I seemed to have a special aptitude for literally "bouncing off the walls." I loved doing cartwheels, flips, and headstands. I didn't know any true application of these skills, but I could do enough to entertain my friends. Somebody would say, "Go stand on your head, Bart," and I would. But learning to do a headstand hadn't just come automatically. The first few times that I tried the trick I had to lean my back against the wall. But on each subsequent effort, I'd try a little harder to be a little quicker or a little straighter. Soon I was confident enough to try it without support.

I was also very physical at school. I was reminded of this when I returned to my old neighborhood after the Olympics. Walking back into that elementary school building was a wonderful experience. I could finally see the tops of the lockers and have those little drinking fountains at my knees. While I was there my kindergarten teacher, Mrs. Miller, told the kids about the day I came to school with no show-and-tell. That may not sound like much now, but when you're in kindergarten, not having your show-and-tell can be a humiliating experience. And so when Mrs. Miller called me to come up to the front of the class, I said, "I don't have a show-and-tell but I can do a headstand." Then I grabbed one of those little nap mats and popped right up. Well, the kids thought this was great! They started counting to see how long I could hold the position. They counted to ten seconds and I was still standing on my head. They counted to thirty seconds and I was still up. Finally, they had counted to one hundred. I loved it. With that much attention, I probably could have stayed there all day. I remember Mrs. Miller saying, "Thank you, Bart, you can come down now—Bart, get down this minute."

Later, when I was in another one of those headstands, somebody said, "Try to push up into a handstand." This sounds simple, but it isn't. It takes a great deal of upper-body strength—the kind of strength that I didn't have at first. But I tried. And I tried it one hundred more times. I fell down, but I always told myself that I was "very-close-to-almost" doing it. And I'd keep on trying a step at a time. There were lots of falls, but I tried to concentrate on the successes—on being *very close*. There's no greater motivation than a little success. Soon I was telling myself, "Hey, I can do this stuff." I forgot the falls and only remembered the end result.

In the fourth grade I took a P.E. class that included a six-week segment on gymnastics. My mom still has a picture of all of us sitting around the floor mat while the instructor tried to teach us tumbling.

As I look at that picture now, all I can see is the arched back on this little kid named Bart. I mean, it's a wonder I didn't crack my vertebrae or something. Still, this clearly represents me in those days: I didn't know anything about the technique of a good gymnastics maneuver, but there I was in front of all of the kids, trying to pull it off.

My P.E. teacher, Les Lange, must have thought I had some potential because one day, toward the end of the six weeks, he took me and my older brother, Bruce, over to see John Burkel and John Armour, gymnastics coaches for Niles West High School. I can still remember every detail of that first visit. The gym was a long, narrow space filled with fluorescent light. There were two levels of bleachers with a balcony and railing forming a belt midway around the room. I could hear squeaking noises and laughter coming from above. We took the stairs to the second level. On one side of the balcony was the gymnastics equipment and on the other side was the wrestling equipment. The balcony bleachers had been folded up against the wall so that the apparatus could be spread around. The floor was covered with big red mats—the kind that take on a hazy look because the custodian scrubs them down every day. Chalk dust was everywhere. Bruce and I stood on the edge of the mats while Mr. Lange went to find the coaches. It was magical. A set of parallel bars was on either side and a guy on the rings was executing an *iron cross* just a few feet in front of us. The area was filled with the members of the high school gymnastics team—tumbling, swinging on the pommel horse, flipping off the high bar. These guys were huge—like giants—and when they hit the mats, loud splats would echo throughout the gym. I looked to my right and watched one of the gymnasts move through his parallel bars routine. As his body swung between the bars his weight caused them to curve like ivory tusks. His knuckles popped out as his hands gripped the wood. With each turn his palms rubbed the bars, causing the squeak that I had heard earlier. He pulled up into a handstand just as Mr. Lange reappeared with Coach Burkel. "Do you want to try some of this?" he asked us. I didn't hesitate for a second. "Sure, I want to try these things," and I headed straight for the parallel bars. They reminded me of the monkey bars in the park, only *much* neater.

A set of parallel bars is eleven feet six inches in length, and usually you work right in the middle. But if you're going to practice a new trick, it's best to do it on the end. That way, if you wipe out, you'll fall on the mats, not the bars. Mr. Lange threw me up to about six inches from the end of the bars and I started swinging back and forth. I thought, *This is easy.* I counted "One, two, three" and I swung up into a handstand. And I held it—the very first time! I held that baby as solid as if I'd been on the floor. The guys on the team stopped what they were doing and came over to watch. I remember hearing one of them say, "What in the devil is *this?*" But I thought it was a snap. After all, at that point I'd been walking up the stairs on my hands and doing handstands on top of the merry-go-round. Those "little rails" were a piece of cake. I flipped off, looked at Coach Burkel, and said, "I love this stuff."

From then on I worked out with the team two nights a week.

When I was eleven, my parents got me my first set of parallel bars. And fitting them into the basement was a squeeze. (One good swing and you'd hit your feet on the ceiling.) Our living room had a cathedral ceiling, and for a few days my parents actually discussed putting the parallel bars in the middle of the room. I remember my dad walking in there one day and saying, "You know, they really would fit in here." Mom vetoed that idea; the bars were put in the backyard along with a pommel horse, and later my dad even hung rings from a tree. My mother was certain that we'd break our necks on those bars, so every once in a while she would cruise the suburbs on a night before a trash pickup, looking for old mattresses. When she'd find one on a sidewalk trash pile, she'd stop and ask if she could take it away. Eventually, it would end up out back, leaning against my p-bars or under the rings.

I was really a show-off in those days. I thought that I could do just about anything. I remember the day I talked my dad into helping me practice a *back handspring*. I had completed my very first one that day in the gym and I couldn't wait to do it again for the "hometown fans." So after dinner, I hustled everybody into the living room with my usual tactics: "Come on, you guys, this is going to be so great, you aren't going to believe it!" When everyone was settled down, I asked my dad to be my assistant. He wasn't so sure about the whole idea, but I begged, "Come on, Dad. I know I can do it. All I need is for somebody to spot me." I showed him how to brace me by putting one of his hands behind my knees and the other along the small of my back. Then I said, "Just throw me up. Give me a start—I can do the rest." But in the gym I had been so excited about doing the flip that I hadn't paid any attention to the coach's role in actually controlling me in the air. And my dad had certainly never spotted flips before. I jumped up and he tried to help, but neither one of us knew what we were doing. I landed square on top of my head. Screaming in pain, I ran to my room, and my mom ran around telling Dad he could have broken my neck. He felt so terrible. I still wonder sometimes if he ever got over the trauma.

After that my dad really got interested in learning a more *constructive* way of helping me with gymnastics. He was right there with me when I competed in my first meet. I was eleven years old. The meet was held in that long, gigantic gymnasium on the Navy Pier in Chicago. There must have been three hundred kids running around in warm-ups and twice that many parents all gathered in the far end of the gym. We competed on the wooden floor, no fancy spring mats like we use today. They just taped off a forty-by-forty-foot square, and we did our routines and banged our heads when we hit the floor. I won two bronze medals: one in floor exercise and another on the rings. What a proud day that was!

Not all my competitive experiences were that victorious. In fact, I was usually the guy who came in second. And as any competitor will tell you, second place is the *worst*. Mark Cameron, National Weightlifting Champion, explained it to me at the '76 Olympics and I thought of it again in '84 when the U.S. Gymnastics Team had been predicted to get a bronze after the Chinese and the Japanese. "Nothing is better than gold, but bronze is second best. When you stand up there on the platform with the bronze, you can look back at all of the other thousands of guys in the pack and say, 'Look at this. I made it up here!' But when you win the silver, people come up to you and say, 'Isn't it too bad that you didn't win.'"

During my elementary school days gymnastics was becoming my favorite sport, but I did other things too. I played halfback on the local Pop Warner football team and I even joined the Cub Scouts (although I did bail out of that long before we hit Eagle Scouts). Sometimes I'd miss a gymnastics practice to play in a football game or I'd miss football practice to stay an extra hour in the gym. I loved football and my coaches probably remember me as the guy who, while still in full uniform, would do backflips along the sidelines. They used to tease me about cartwheeling through the line. I never scored a touchdown, but if I had, I could have done some awesome tricks in the end zone!

After I had been in gymnastics a couple of years, Coach Burkel felt that I needed to also work out with kids my own age. The high school guys were a fantastic challenge for me, and I continued working with them, but Coach said that I should learn where I fit in with my chronological peers. So I began a second training program at the Evanston Y.M.C.A., and later a third at the Northwest Suburban Y.M.C.A.

This was a wonderful experience for me, because I got a chance to see how I was improving and thus gain some real confidence. It was good in another way because I wasn't *the* best kid in the program. Tim Slottow was eleven months younger than I and he was also fantastic, strong, a brilliant gymnast, articulate, from a very wealthy family, and so good-looking that the girls all loved him. He beat me every time. Up until that point I had been the star— then there was Tim.

Still, we had some terrific times traveling together as teammates and bringing home boxes of trophies from every meet. He'd always win first and I'd always win second. I can remember only one time, at a little meet in Canton, Ohio, that I was able to beat Tim.

When the U.S. Men's Gymnastic Team competed in Chicago against the top European champions, the meet organizers brought in Tim Slottow to do an exhibition—that's how amazing he was. I wasn't that good and I didn't get invited to participate in the exhibition—all I could do was watch. And it hurt. But it also made me work harder than ever. I tried to turn my feelings of envy and competition into something constructive. And in the end my weaknesses helped me, while Tim's strengths came to victimize him. Because he was *so* physically advanced and talented, he was pushed. By everybody. They'd ask him to do stunts, and because he could, they'd ask him to do something a little harder. The result was a severe problem with the growth plates in the disks of his back. He spent several years in a back brace and rarely competed.

One of the most exciting times for me in the early days was when I took my first "road trip." It was 1971. The coaches piled our little team into a big old station wagon and we all drove to Des Moines, Iowa, to compete at the Cornerhouse Y.M.C.A. At the meet there must have been eighty or a hundred boys at all age levels. Tim Slottow won the overall title, but this time, I took third place. A funny little kid that I'd never seen before beat me out of second. He had this big round head with short-cropped hair and the most enormous ears I had ever seen. I sneaked around behind him and took a picture of the back of his head, just so I could show those ears to my friends back home. It was Jim Hartung. And in the following years he was to become my fierce collegiate competitor in the rivalries of Nebraska and Oklahoma, my Olympic teammate in Los Angeles, and a very good friend.

There were hundreds of meets after that. I competed in crowded stadiums and in empty old gyms. Once I remember taking a swing on the high bar, looking at the gym clock, and noticing that it was 12:25 A.M.! It was one of those meets in which there were too many boys scheduled and the judges took too long with the scoring. But I didn't care—I was on and it was "showtime." (Now officials have prevented such scenes. Junior meets must be terminated by 10:00 P.M., even if there are competitions still in progress.)

One year my dad accompanied me to the Y.M.C.A. Junior finals outside of New Orleans. There were about three or four guys and about eighteen girls representing the Northwest Suburban Y.M.C.A. We began the competitions at 10:00 A.M. the first morning and we spent more than two and a half days in that gym. We'd sit there for hours, compete a little, eat our cheeseburgers in the stands, and then trudge back to the hotel. My dad thought that this was tragic. "We're in *New Orleans* and for once, you kids are going to see something other than the gym," he said. There were more than twenty of us, but my dad had a plan. He loaded up one car, shuttled it downtown, left that group with the girls' chaperon, and ferried back and forth until we were all standing on Bourbon Street. I was twelve. There we were with our little warm-ups and gym bags, moving down the French Quarter, tripping over winos in the street, trying to peek into the strip joints—what a trip!

After that, every trip became more than a gymnastics meet. When we went to New York, for example, my dad took me to a Broadway play. When we went to Strasbourg, we sat on the banks of the Rhine.

By the time I was in junior high school, homework and gymnastics occupied a lot of my time, but I still had all of the normal adolescent experiences: I worked hard at getting the other kids to like me, I sat in the park with my girlfriend and listened to "our" song (Diana Ross's "Ain't No Mountain High Enough"), and I tried to look like one of the Beatles (which is no easy trick when you're a green-eyed blond). I even let my friends talk me into running for a class office. Never entering into anything halfheartedly, I threw myself into the campaign. I gathered a core of loyal supporters, went throughout the school talking to everybody, made posters, and passed out buttons. My opponent turned out to be one of my best friends and so when I went to the polls, I thought that I should vote for him. It seemed like the right thing to do. I lost by two votes. Mine and his.

Meanwhile, I was back into my sport. For many years junior gymnastics competitions had been directed by the Amateur Athletics Union (AAU). But in 1972 the United States Gymnastics Federation (USGF) was organized to challenge the AAU over which would be the governing body for gymnastics in this country. USGF approached the International Gymnastics Federation and asked for the opportunity to sponsor major gymnastics meets. So from 1972 until about 1975, there were two simultaneous rounds of competition. Eventually, the USGF won out, and now the AAU has little to do with gymnastics. But in 1972, at Spokane, Washington, I won my first national competition, the AAU Junior Olympics.

Then in 1974, at the age of sixteen, I entered the first USGF Junior National Championships. It was held in Algonquin, Illinois, on a very hot summer day. When we got to the meet, we learned that it was to be held outside on a field—just like the old-time gymnastics tournaments. At that time the technical director of the USGF was three-time Olympian Frank Cumiskey. Cumiskey remembered gymnastics as it was in Berlin—on a field in front of Hitler. To him, gymnastics meant outdoors. I thought my dad was going to have a coronary, right on the spot. It seemed like a neat idea to me—the sun was shining, everything looked great. But I had forgotten for a second about my dad's engineering background. After a few hours of the sun beating down on the equipment, the surface temperatures approached "a million degrees." The mats were boiling, and between competitions we had to keep towels on the high bar so that the guys could hold on to it. A garbage dump was in the next field, and just before I was to go up on my high bar routine, the dump caught fire. There I was whipping around the bar for all I was worth and catching glimpses of my dad beating out that fire with a piece of mat.

Later in the competition we even recruited Dad to weigh down the vaulting horse for us. Good ol' Dad.

I took first place in that meet, Tiger Taylor from Tallahassee, Florida, was second, and a little kid named Kurt Thomas took third. Another little kid who took first place in the age group just below us was Jim Mikus, our alternate for the 1984 U.S. Olympic Team.

In order to encourage us all to enter this first meet, the USGF offered to take the winners of the top two age groups when the U.S. National Men's Team traveled abroad. That year the team traveled to two international meets, one in South Africa and one in Varna, Bulgaria, for the World Championships. Mikus went to South Africa and I ended up in Bulgaria. But not because of the USGF. After I had won, they lost some funding and defaulted on their promise. My parents decided that I had earned the trip, so they paid for me to accompany the Men's National Team. I was allowed to train and practice with the team—everything but compete.

During the month we stayed in Bulgaria, I met and talked with all of the international gymnastics stars. Before leaving home, I had taken my life's savings—$167.34—and purchased a Bauer movie camera so that I could film the practice sessions and warm-ups. When I got back, I had my own library of the most advanced gymnastics techniques being practiced anywhere in the world. Not everybody on our National Men's Team knew the competitors like I did. They'd look at a team like the Japanese and just refer to them as "The Japanese Team." Not me. I studied every one of those guys. I knew Kajiyama and I knew Tsukahara. And I memorized every move in Eizo Kenmotsu's floor routine. The next time I saw the international gymnasts I was just "one of the guys."

The experience was good for me from a social and cultural standpoint as well. In a month you can learn just about all you'd ever want to know about Bulgaria. I found the whole place to be pretty grim. The people were sullen and slow moving. They seemed to just be angry and bitter at life in general. I learned to speak a little of the language, but even then going into a shop or a restaurant was a chore. You could sit at your table for forty-five minutes before anybody would come over to ask what you wanted. It wasn't just because I was an American, the Bulgarians weren't even nice to their own people.

I graduated from high school in 1976, and it's safe to say that I was "heavily committed" to gymnastics. By that time I had already won the AAU Junior National Championship, the USGF Junior National Championship, a Co-championship of the USGF Senior Nationals, been a member of the U.S. Pan-Am Team, and represented the United States in Montreal's 1976 Olympic Games.

It took me almost eight years to complete my degree at Oklahoma University, and not because I was a slow student. Between the '76 Olympics and the '84 Olympics I trained for and competed in: the World University Games in Varna, Bulgaria; the World Championships in Strasbourg; the World Cup in São Paulo; another World Cup in Tokyo; The Champions All competition in London; the World Championships in Fort Worth; the 1980 American Olympic team trials; the World Championships in Moscow; the World Championships in Budapest; as well as numerous United States and NCAA championships throughout the country.

These competitions gave me opportunities few kids my age

could enjoy. For instance, I had traveled to China three times before I was twenty-four years old. (Did you know that in some of the rural provinces they routinely serve fried baby sparrows with dinner—just like we serve mashed potatoes? I always lost weight in China!) I also had opportunities to see foreign competitors outside of the arenas.

At every competition the athletes from each country enjoy time with one another. We go out to dinner, see the sights, or just hang around in the gym, learning one another's tricks. The exceptions, of course, are those athletes from the Eastern Bloc. It's harder for them because they are surrounded by their secret police. Some secret—they travel with these big fat guys dressed in warm-ups who have been introduced as the *trainers.* I remember when I first met Nadia Comaneci and one of her "coaches." This guy had a baggy warm-up suit and a three-day beard. When he wasn't right next to her, she'd nod toward him and roll her eyes as if to say, "Look at this loser over here." The athletes are usually just like the rest of us.

The first time that I ever got to *really* meet the Russians was in 1977 during the Coca-Cola Invitational in Brighton, England. Jim Hartung, Mike Wilson (an '80 Olympian and my teammate at Oklahoma University), and I were the "kids" on the American team. (Mike and I were nineteen and Hartung was about seventeen.) After the meet, there was a big formal banquet, and after the banquet, the athletes were sent to their rooms so the coaches could all go back down to the bar. On the way out, one of the Russians motioned for some of us to follow him.

We slipped around the halls for a while and after the coaches had left, we knocked on the door to this guy's room. When we got inside, the whole Russian men's team was there, sitting around on the furniture and drinking vodka. This place was a pit. There were empty vodka bottles, and fruit, big loaves of bread, clothes, and stereo equipment all over everything. Of course, they weren't supposed to have any of this stuff, but they had taken their food ration money, sneaked a guy out to a "take-away" liquor store for vodka, sneaked another out to a stereo shop, and so on. They had packed away quite a little warehouse. What they wanted from us were American jeans. New ones with the tags still on them brought the highest price, $200. Old jeans were worth about $50. In 1977 fifty bucks for a pair of jeans seemed like quite a deal. How they planned to get all of that stuff back into Russia they didn't say and we didn't ask.

They were terrific guys, laughing and singing and chanting *nosdarovia*. They pulled out water glasses, filled them with warm vodka, and gave us each one. I looked at Jim, he looked at me. Hartung sniffed his glass and said, "I think this stuff is airplane fuel." Out of the sheer power of international diplomacy, we drank the stuff—ugh! We used sign language to talk about the meet, we swapped pictures of girlfriends, and finally we went back to our rooms to get them some American clothes.

They were like this when you saw them away from their guards, but, of course, they couldn't act very friendly to us in public. They really had to walk a tight line. If they did anything to show sympathy or interest for the West, they probably wouldn't have been allowed to come out again.

Life can be very hard for an athlete or a coach in such a restrictive political system. Certainly they're not allowed to pursue their personal freedoms, and this impacts upon the choices they can make as athletes. Sometimes their governments actually decide which sport each athlete may specialize in.

And, usually, Communist governments won't allow family members to travel together when athletes tour western countries. Defection simply becomes too attractive. One notable exception occurred in 1981 and the result probably caused restrictions to tighten even more. Bela Karolyi and his wife were both allowed to leave the East as coaches for the Romanian women's team. After leaving their eight-year-old daughter with her aunt, they defected to the United States. They came to stay with Coach Ziert and me in Oklahoma, and in an attempt to retrieve their daughter, we petitioned any senator and congressman who would listen to us. Finally, we found a sympathetic ear with Congressman Bill Archer, a member of the committee renegotiating Romania's economic contract for Most Favored Nation status. Release of the Karolyis' daughter became an unspoken part of the bargain.

(Currently Bela is making some significant improvements in our women's gymnastics program. All of us have already seen the talents of his latest star, Mary Lou Retton.)

Meeting international gymnasts and traveling all over the world has been a truly exciting adventure—not to mention what it has done for my souvenir collection. At most national and international meets athletes are given a large souvenir gym bag. I stuffed all the extra bags under my bed until they caused it to rise off the ground.

Throughout all of the growth, adventure, and excitement of those early years, my family was a strong and supportive element of my success. I remember when I was five and wanted my first pair of racing skates. My mom had already established what she called her "Olympic fund." Any extra change or odd-job money she earned went into the fund and was used to buy skates, lessons, and millions of sweat socks for me and my brothers. My parents also sacrificed greater amounts of money when it was necessary to accompany me all over the world. (Heaven only knows how much they've spent on film alone!) But through it all, we were always told that athletics was a family project—something important for everyone.

I also know that my competitive spirit and drive have grown because of the example of my brothers. I guess that all three of us were pretty "determined." My brother Bruce always wanted to be a commercial airline pilot, but when he was young, a doctor told him that because he wore glasses, there was no way. That certainly wasn't enough to make Bruce give up! He stuck with his dream, always taking classes and developing skills that would eventually help him to fly. Later, the advances in optometry and changes in FAA regulations permitted pilots with certain types of corrected vision. Bruce is now a pilot for Sunworld Airways.

My younger brother, Michael, is undoubtedly the most gregarious of us all. And while he, like Bruce, was a national speed skater, his biggest goal was to excel in something that his brothers hadn't. So he became a fantastic musician, the captain of his soccer team, and went to work on his electrical engineering degree.

Now that the three of us have survived childhood, our parents have been able to breathe a little easier. They moved from Illinois to my dad's home state of Oklahoma, where he joined the faculty of Oklahoma University's School of Environmental Design. Meanwhile, Mom has become a management consultant. It surprised no one that after raising us, she would specialize in employee motivation. We like telling people the story about Mom and Princess, one of the family dogs. A few years ago a veterinarian told my mother that there was no way that our seven-year-old dog could be walking. Her hip joints were severely arthritic and yet Princess accompanied Mom on a daily three-mile walk. "Lady, you've just got a motivated dog," he said. My mother replied, "I've got motivated *everything*."

Bart has accomplished a great deal for a young man of twenty-seven. And the foundation he received from his family and first coaches has been with him throughout this experience. He displays concern for other people, self-confidence, and an ability to set goals and execute tasks. All of these traits are the direct result of his early contact with strong and caring adults.

But parents and coaches are only a part of the story. The most significant factor leading to Bart's success is Bart himself. This becomes apparent when you recognize his physical strengths *and* weaknesses. If you were to design the perfect gymnastic machine, you would include great flexibility in the shoulders and back, and the ability to execute powerful and explosive tumbling moves. Although Bart has many fine gymnastic qualities, he is not particularly strong in any of these essential areas.

A most primary example of such "physical weakness" is Bart's relative lack of spinal flexibility. One very minor trick that is unnecessary for competitive gymnastics but which illustrates back flexibility is the *front limber*. In this maneuver the athlete must kick up to a handstand, go over into a back bend, and then pull up. It took Bart over three years to accomplish this feat. And that was *after* he had won several national gymnastics championships. Many young children perform this same trick after a month of instruction.

Additionally, when he came to me after high school, his tumbling skills were relatively low. He could not execute one of the most fundamental elite tumbling maneuvers, the *double backflip*. Although he can now most certainly do a *double backflip* on the floor, he does not tumble off the ceiling—explode in the air—the way someone like the great Li Ning of China does.

Given the cold, mechanical facts—considering the physics of our sport—Bart *shouldn't be able* to perform at the highest levels of international competition. He is not "physically designed" to do it. But he does. And he wins.

It took me a long time to verbalize this. He had accomplished so much as a beginning gymnast that I couldn't bring myself to say out loud, "Hey, what's going on here? This kid is not very physically talented. How does he do this stuff?" His physical limitations as a competitive gymnast were most apparent in the floor exercises event. But like all champions, Bart seemed to work the hardest on this, his weakest point. As a result, he has become an excellent tumbler. In fact, he has been a finalist in floor exercise in nearly every international competition since 1979.

Bart loves his sport and he loves to achieve. As a result, he uses hard work, determination, and will to more than compensate for his physical shortcomings.

CHAPTER 2

Nothing Motivates
Like a Little Success
—Becoming a Champion

More than one person has said to me, "Where did you get the desire to succeed?" or "What makes you want to be a champion?" And I've wondered about it myself. Desire can be a combination of so many individual factors and characteristics, but for me it seems to rest with a few simple principles:

- Enjoy what you are doing.
- Expect only the best from yourself.
- Learn to define goals—both short range and long range.
- Be willing to trust your instincts and feelings even if they contradict reason and logic.

Chance can allow you to accomplish a goal once in a while, but consistent achievement happens only if you love what you are doing. Gymnastics is hard and often tedious work—but I've always made what I *have* to do into something that I *want* to do. For example, instead of concentrating on how miserable it can be to do *handstand push-ups,* I think about how I want to perform when I go out there on the floor. I want people to feel something— to enjoy an action or movement—almost as much as if they were doing it themselves. If I were a singer or a stand-up comic, you would say that I was a "ham." I can't do a *straddle "L"* support on the parallel bars if I have not maintained the muscle strength of my upper arms. So instead of thinking about the push-ups, I think about how I love to perform.

The second quality that can make a champion is drive or ambition. I am always striving to be better than I've ever been. If you win a meet and you know that the other guys were off or that you "slopped along," that's not a real win. But if you go out there one day and top yourself—do the best routine, the most creative routine you've ever done—then you've won. Even if you scored at the back of the pack.

It's not that I'm not satisfied with the things I've accomplished. I do sincerely enjoy looking back with pleasure and even pride. But that doesn't last very long. I remember reading an article once where a sports psychologist said athletes should be awarded apples and bananas instead of trophies and medals. He claimed their trophies just collect dust and remind people of the past. If the first place award were a banana, an athlete could eat and enjoy the banana for a short time and then get on to the next goal. There's always something else ahead.

What I honestly don't know is where my "hunger" came from. I don't know if my desire is inherited or learned. As I mentioned earlier, I have a very supportive family. They've backed me in anything I've wanted to do and they've encouraged wide horizons. For instance, I've always been interested in automobiles. And I remember when my father said, "Why don't you plan on being the president of Ford Motor Company someday." I mean, that's how my parents are—nothing seems too farfetched!

They didn't just talk about possibilities, they also taught me the mechanics of how to make something work. When I was in high school, I hated Calculus class. And if I came home with a problem out of my reach, it would usually take on the proportions of a national crisis. I'd rant around for a while; rave that it was a stupid class. But my dad would calmly sit down with me and say, "Okay, what is your goal here? What are you trying to accomplish in this assignment? Just find one thing you enjoy about the class and we'll go from there."

This technique for solving problems is pretty straightforward. Just ask yourself a few simple questions: What do I want? What actions are necessary for getting it? What is the most logical and most direct sequence in which these actions must occur? What people can help me? How can I accomplish step one?

Initially, it's hard to identify something that you truly want. Your priorities can become confused amid all of the choices and opportunities available to you. That's why it's so important for you to explore as many possibilities as you can. (Obviously, gymnastics became a major goal for me, but I had tried many sports and activities before I made that decision.) Finally, you must evaluate the worthiness of your goal. For me, gymnastics met the moral standards my parents had taught me—it was enjoyable, it was beneficial to me, and it didn't hurt anyone else.

One of the first major gymnastics goals to present a challenge for me was learning the *stutz* (a movement in which the gymnast changes direction on the parallel bars). When I was fourteen, I said to Coach Burkel, "In three and a half weeks I'm going to jump up on those p-bars and perform the *stutz*." That was setting my goal. With the coach's help and the guidance of one of my heros, Bob Manna, I literally listed those things necessary to execute the maneuver. Every day I worked on the plan step-by-step. In two and a half weeks I had done it.

My coach used to tell me to think of goal setting as a long paved road. Your major goal is at the end of the road, miles away. There are many side roads, detours, and intersections. It's okay to explore and even drift off the road. But as long as you always point in the right direction, and as long as your detours return to the main road, you'll reach your goal.

The final step in goal achievement is the easiest to verbalize and the most difficult to execute. The best plan means nothing until you "go for it." In gymnastics we refer to it with a Japanese word, *gamba.* The Japanese have been leaders in our sport for many years, and when you visit a gym in their country, you hear the athletes calling to one another, *"Gamba desu!"* But the term has more of a spiritual feeling for the Japanese. It means "Go for it. We're with you; we believe in you. This is the right thing." At some time you must be able and willing to say, "This is important to me and I'm going full blast. I'm willing to commit time, energy, or whatever it takes to reach this goal."

The most advanced expression of this commitment to "go for it" involves taking risks. I had been in gymnastics for ten years before I learned that lesson. Up until that time I was known as a gymnast who was capable of executing "perfect mechanics." I had all of the fundamentals down pat. I did all of the "little things" very well. That is what I had been taught, and that is what I did. In 1978 that strategy had put me in the parallel bars finals of the World Championships, and making those finals was my breakthrough as an international competitor. Eizo Kenmotsu was the reigning champion of the event. I had been in other major meets, but so had all of the other guys. Being in the finals of the World Championships was different and I felt like quite a hotshot little gymnast. I stepped up to the bars, did my usual, safe routine, and scored a 9.85. Talk about feeling on top of the world! I was sure that that was it! At the end of the finals I was in fifth place. On the way home Coach Ziert said to me, "You know, Bart, you were just as good as anybody there. You could have won it—but you didn't do anything *special.*"

He was right. I had done a pretty fair job; I had done everything "by the textbook." And all I got was a polite "Thank you very much. Come again next year." This had been the event in which Kenmotsu introduced a fantastic new maneuver, the *giant swing*. All of us who saw it were "knocked out." That's why he was the champ.

Back in the gym I had a new goal: finding something special for my routine. The first problem was finding something that would be different, that would be exciting, and that wouldn't break my neck. I was just about to give up when, one day, still in my practice warm-ups, I got an idea. I pressed to a handstand on one rail. It was totally new—I'd never seen anybody do it before. Earlier I had discovered that while most other guys mounted the bars through the center, I was able to mount from the side. It didn't mean much by itself, but when I followed it with a full *pirouette* (a 360-degree turn), a swing between the bars, and then pressed up to that handstand on one bar, we had ourselves a whole new ballgame.

My next event was a collegiate meet in Ames, Iowa. My team, Oklahoma University, was competing against the University of Nebraska and Iowa State. I was so excited about my new routine that I could hardly wait my turn. I mounted the bars, started the maneuver, and fell off. My score was 8.75. I used the trick in two subsequent meets and I fell off in both of them. All of a sudden I wasn't getting my usual 9.7s or 9.8s, I was getting 9.3 or even 9.0.

Even my parents—my most ardent supporters—were asking, "What's happening, Bart, you used to be pretty good?"

But Coach Ziert kept insisting, "It'll work. One day, I promise, it will work."

In 1979 the World Championships were held in Ft. Worth, Texas. I included my special new maneuvers in the routine, and guess who won the parallel bars?

You've got it! Me! I'd finally learned to take a chance and go for it.

The mechanics of problem-solving have become so automatic that now, when something is important to me, I feel that I know how to make it work. This skill may be one of the greatest gifts that I have received from my parents. But *real* self-confidence—

the conviction that I could tackle absolutely anything—that was something I had to learn for myself.

My dad's a professor of engineering and his viewpoint on life has always been pure logic. He is incredibly skillful at analysis, methodical plotting, and step-by-step execution. No problem is ever so big that my dad can't compute all variables, set a goal, and get to work. Every task is simply set out in a series of small tasks. Yet there are times when he almost makes it seem *too* easy. In many situations it is true that if you can make a logical plan and then work it through, there is the result. And my dad taught me how to execute and achieve in this manner. But often as a task becomes more complex, it consists of more and more variables that are out of your control. It's no longer a simple matter of your executing a straightforward little plan. I can remember being so offended when, as an "aspiring" Olympian, people would say to me, "Bart, we just *know* that you're going to win an Olympic medal someday. It just *has* to be." Well—it *didn't* have to be. I could have skillfully executed every aspect of a *plan* and there could still have been a thousand factors preventing my success. I was furious that some people expected me to have control over *everything*.

It's true that your life can be organized by goals or by a list of pros and cons. Decisions should be made within a logical frame of reference, but sometimes you've got to reach beyond that. I vividly remember the time in my life when I made this discovery. I was graduating from high school as a world-class gymnastics champion. Obviously, I was happy that my life was going in that direction. It was time to select a collegiate program that would further enhance my skills and competitive stamina.

There was also a career decision to be made. I had always been interested in mechanics—things like how the lawn mower worked and how airplanes fly. I was also a good math and science student. Since Dad was an engineer, the natural choice was for me to become an engineer as well.

And so I began looking at schools with both gymnastics and engineering programs. There were some fantastic collegiate gymnastics programs available and I was approached by many coaches who wanted me to join their teams. I made long lists of the pros and cons of each school as I tried to make a choice. I remember sitting with a dozen or so such lists detailing the relative merits of schools like Louisiana State University, the University of Michigan, Pennsylvania State University, the University of California at Berkeley, Southern Illinois University, the University of Oregon, and Iowa State.

Finally, I said, "Wait a minute. Here I am trying to organize one of the most important decisions of my life based upon logic and facts—but what I really want to do is go to Oklahoma University." This was not a logical conclusion. While all of those other schools had top-ranking gymnastics programs—the biggest facilities, the most successful coaches, the most Olympians—Oklahoma University was ranked nineteenth in the NCAA. But I had a gut reaction, an intuition that Oklahoma was where I *wanted* to be. Not where I *logically* should have gone, but where I *wanted* to be. Primarily, I liked the coach at Oklahoma. I had first heard of Paul Ziert when he was training gymnasts at a high school in Chicago. But before we could meet, he left to become head coach for Oklahoma University. Two summers later I attended a Junior National training camp and Ziert was one of the staff members. He had a tremendous energy and love of the sport, but more importantly, I thought that he was the most creative gymnastic coach I had ever seen. He had an excellent knowledge of the technical side of gymnastics, but he didn't try to impress us with all of the usual "coach jargon." Rather, he talked to us about *thinking through* and *feeling* the movements in our routines. He talked to us about things other than mere mechanics.

Pitching out my logical lists and going to Oklahoma was a monumental step for me because, more than making an important decision about which coach would be directing my gymnastics future, I was deciding to think for myself. Right or wrong, I knew what I wanted to do. And I did it.

My decision to work with Coach Ziert prompted two of my Illinois teammates, Craig Martin and Les Moore, to join us. The very next spring we tied for first place in the NCAA Gymnastics Championships. We had a hot little team going, and the second year we won the NCAA title free and clear.

Now I have no hesitancy when I experience a gut-level contradiction to logic. I listen to and trust what my feelings tell me.

This crossroads was also essential to my success or "winning" in gymnastics. When I made this choice, I became independent. And actually, you could say that it was here that I became an adult. But the decision helped me to mature in my sport as well. Gymnastics isn't just mechanics, it is also emotion. When you are performing tricks and routines for an audience you can't fake it. You can know the mechanics and you can be a highly trained athlete, but your emotions—and the ability to express them to an audience—that's what makes a gymnastics champion. And making the decision about which college to attend was the first time in my entire life that I had allowed emotion to become an important part of my character.

The Coach's Side

Bart's real talent is the way he leads our sport in artistic expression and originality. In most major competitions, he has performed new routines. Not all gymnasts do this. Many of them simply reperform comfortable material.

Bart is aware of a most important principle of the sport and of life—you have to take a chance if you are to pull away from the "pack" of competent people. There are lots of people who perform a set of tasks at a very competent, correct level. Always the same way, always correctly. If you ask them to march out there on the floor and perform a trick one hundred times, ninety-nine times they will perform it *perfectly*. Only a few individuals seem willing to risk stretching for something beyond that. Bart reaches, and I think that another American gymnast who also does this is Mitch

Gaylord. Risk-taking can be disastrous. One slight error and you can, as the gymnasts say, "wipe out." But when such a gymnast hits, then he's truly spectacular.

Much of Bart's skill rests in the way he uses his personality to present a new routine to the judges. But before this can be executed, the routine must be created. It usually begins with a loony idea. A few years ago we created a floor exercise routine in which he did a front flip, and landed—not on his feet, as usual—but on his knees. When he first performed the trick, people in the audience couldn't believe it. It was so outrageous and so unexpected that they thought we were crazy. However, it not only earned him points, it earned him the respect of the gymnastics community.

A more recent example occurred with the combination that is a part of his Olympic parallel bars routine. First he did a *stutz*. This is a relatively common trick in which the gymnast swings down between the bars, swings up, turns, and ends up in a *handstand* facing the opposite direction. Bart is the first person who dared in competition to complete that *handstand* with his legs straddled. In conventional judging a straddled or open leg position in a *handstand* is an automatic form deduction. But since he did it in such an obvious and intentional manner, it became a new maneuver.

But Bart's most spectacular bit of creativity resulted in the *Conner Spin*, a move that distinguishes his parallel bar routine from all others. After the *straddled stutz*, he does a full *pirouette* (turn)—still in straddle—moves to a split position, comes down on one bar to the *straddle "L" position*, does another *pirouette* on that one bar, holds the position, and then finally presses to a one-bar *handstand*. On the day we were creating that sequence we were visited in the gym by our friend Andy Olson. Andy is the Director of Marketing Services for Caesars Palace in Las Vegas, and after the workout, he said, "Thank you for letting me share that. It was wonderful to witness that kind of gymnastics creativity."

CHAPTER 3

Make Something You Have to Do Something You Want to Do
—Setting Goals

What frustrates me now is that when people think of gymnastics, they think only of the Olympics. That episode is just one specific goal at the end of one specific path. The Olympics constituted a very important week of my life, there's no doubt about it. But it's the other fifteen years of pleasure in step-by-step accomplishment that define gymnastics for me.

When people talk to me about the sport, they want to hear about Los Angeles, 1984. And often they specifically want to know if their kids can make it in some future Olympics. This presents special problems for me. When I see a kid in the fourth grade who's five feet two inches tall and weighs one hundred and fifty pounds, I just know that he probably won't become an Olympic gymnast.

The sport has evolved in such a way that in order to compete on the highest levels, you must possess specific physical characteristics. These would include an upper-body strength in greater proportion to body weight, balance, overall flexibility, hand/eye coordination, and long arms. There are even many doctors who believe there is a specific type of muscle tissue (it's called fast twitch or explosive fiber) that would be of little help to a marathon runner but is essential for a quick, intense sport like gymnastics.

I'm really not comfortable saying that to parents. And I *never* say it to kids starting out in the sport. If parents come to me with a fifteen-year-old daughter who's been in gymnastics for four months, I'm not going to tell them that they're wasting their time. After all, the physical benefits of a regular exercise program, the mental stamina of team competition, and especially the sheer joy of gymnastics will still be available to her, even though the Olympics will not. Almost every day I'll sign an autograph for a parent who will say something like "My son started gymnastics Wednesday and he's going to win a gold medal in the year 2004." My answer is always positive, because I believe that if you want it, you should go for it. But it hurts me to think that already this kid and this parent have a goal that is a hundred years away. What is he going to miss on the way there? Unless he truly enjoys meeting every small challenge, he won't make it.

A young person entering gymnastics must accept reality. For example, I am the current Olympic gold medalist in the parallel bars. The *only* one. And if I'm going to sign autographs for kids who also aspire to this goal, then I've got to do *more* than just smile and say, "Go for it, kid." Somewhere, at sometime, I've got a responsibility to remind those same kids that there're a lot of people standing in line to knock me off. I've got a similar responsibility to show them the rewards and satisfactions that can be theirs at any level of the sport.

I have a plaque on my bedroom wall that reads, "There's nothing wrong with chasing dreams, you just might catch one." I believe that it's important to set spectacular goals, to know the major

35

Make
Something
You Have
to Do
Something
You Want
to Do

directions you want for yourself. But your day-to-day existence is maintained only by the small dreams, like going for a bit more extension in a stretch, or getting a little higher in the next jump. Or maybe you'll say to yourself, "I'm going to learn that cartwheel by Friday." This was the most important lesson that I learned from my first gymnastics coach, John Burkel.

Coach Burkel taught me another important lesson, about learning in the proper sequence. Once, when I was about eleven, I was assigned to work on a beginning move on the high bar, a *kip*. (It's a move in which you jerk your body from below the bar to a position above the bar.) But I decided that I would rather learn an advanced high bar maneuver called the *giant swing*. While the coach was working with somebody on the other side of the gym, I practiced and practiced this second trick on my own. When he came over, I proudly cast up into the *giant* and swung all the way around the bar. I must admit, it was unusual for a kid my age to have accomplished this skill. Coach Burkel calmly said, "Bart, that was very good, but I don't ever want to see you do that until you learn to do your *kip*. You will have lots of exciting experiences with difficult moves, but in the meantime, you can't skip over a fundamental move like the *kip*. Learn to do it well so that you develop your fundamentals first, then the big tricks will be easy."

Throughout those early years I never said, "I want to be an Olympic champion." Rather, I would say something like "Next May I want to compete in a meet in St. Louis. In June, I want to be in a meet in Michigan." Before I realized it, something as far away as the Olympic trials was right there in front of me. What would have been a dream in the beginning was actually an obtainable goal. It was just as real at this point as was that long-ago "Friday" when I had finally learned the cartwheel.

Gymnastics is an individual sport, but it cannot be done alone. The athlete must execute skills, but he will be judged upon how he *appears* to others, and for this, he needs another's eyes. Bart never scoffs at an instruction or a coaching decision. He will always give it a try. This lack of prejudgment makes my work a pleasure. That's certainly not the case with all gymnasts. Recently I worked with another young athlete, one who was *much* more physically talented than Bart, but one whose attitude will probably prevent him from becoming a champion. I would tell this kid to try a new, perhaps unusual skill, and his response was always the same. "Why do you want me to do that?" Frankly, this attitude can make a coach lose interest. It's different with Bart. He has a way of making you *want* to coach him. I don't know what else to call it but respect. He respects himself so much that he's not afraid to respect you as well. He also knows how to get your professional attention. And it's not because he's so talented. Every coach wants to work with the most physically superior athletes. You can teach them a trick in thirty seconds—and they can do it, pure and simple. You can't do that with Bart. It takes a while for him to coax his body to respond correctly. But all the while his mental attributes—his personality, his determination, his creativity and humor— simply make you *want* to help him succeed.

I've spent a great deal of time trying to analyze exactly how he does this and I believe it is a skill composed of two elements. First, he gives you his undivided attention. I mean, eyeball to eyeball. When we are discussing a routine, the walls of the gym could fall down, and if I continued to talk, he would still be concentrating on what I was saying. He rarely allows himself to become the focus of this attention— it's always the other person. Simply put, he makes you feel important.

Secondly, he is so task-committed that he takes direction extremely well. Once he feels that you know what you're

37

Make
Something
You Have
to Do
Something
You Want
to Do

doing, and once he knows the plan of action, he's off. For example, soon after the Olympics, Bart had an opportunity to work with Michael Landon in the television series *Highway to Heaven*. Bart, going into that project, respected Landon's acting, directing, and producing expertise. And so when he was on the set, he watched Landon's every move, paid attention, and completed every task exactly as he was directed to do. The result was that instead of an athlete portraying himself, the audience saw a real dramatic performance. And this was from a young man who had never acted before in his life.

I think that Bart's skill in this area is something that a lot of us can identify with and use to define our own personal goals. Give someone your full attention, try to do what that individual needs to have done, and he or she will do almost anything to *help* you succeed.

Giving your full attention and following directions both require two distinctly different qualities: tremendous self-confidence and vulnerability. The self-confidence seems obvious—you must trust in your ability to execute tasks. But in addition, you must be vulnerable or open to the ideas and emotions of others.

My current coach, Paul Ziert, and I run a gymnastics club in Norman, Oklahoma. At the club we work with kids aged three to eighteen, some of whom have been taking tumbling for five or six years. With great enthusiasm they practice back handsprings and cartwheels. They may never compete on an Olympic level, but they have already gained a great deal. These are the kids who have acquired tumbling skills which can get them selected to the cheerleading squad, or who have acquired mental skills identical to those needed for long-term academic projects. Finally, they have developed balance, muscle strength, and flexibility. These are the physical skills that can become the basis for general life-long sports activities or that can become the foundation for other competitive sports experiences. Olympic wrestler Mark Shultz, for example, was once a State Champion in gymnastics. Sugar Ray Leonard of boxing fame started as a gymnast. Laura McCloy, a National Champion in the sport of cross-country running, lives down the street from me. Every time I see her, she reminds me of how important early gymnastics training was to her development as a runner.

But more than that, gymnastics is a "whole-body" sport. It requires your total body, mind, and spirit. It's no accident that the Chinese and the Japanese are fantastic gymnasts. Yes, it's true that their ethnic body structure—strength and size proportions—has a great deal to do with their facility on gymnastics equipment. But it's more than that. Eastern philosophies have always focused upon this "harmony of body, mind, and spirit," and Oriental gymnasts seem to understand and respect this relationship. Because of the discipline required for the sport—I mean, nobody *wants* to get up every morning for two hours of routine calisthenics—a relationship between your mind and your body is readily apparent. Philosophy becomes reality when you have to *use* your mind to force your legs up for one more lift. There are times when I fall on the mat and say, "I just can't do any more." But my mind forces me on. Sometimes it's an obvious goal—like when I don't want to climb up on the exercise bicycle and I remind myself of the next meet. Regardless of what you tell yourself, you've got to make your mind and body *work* together if you have any hopes for achievement.

Some people have more difficulty with this task than do others. In the case of a ten-year-old who dreads going to the gym for a workout, the reasons for this can be complex. Maybe his parents are forcing him to do something, assuming it'll be good for him and forgetting to get him involved in the initial decision. Everybody recognizes what's been called the "Little League syndrome." Mom wants a little "Mary Lou Retton" or Dad wants a son he can play ball with. Maybe the child dreads the workout because his coach has never shown him how to set small goals and so he's overwhelmed by the big ones, which seem so distant.

Earlier I mentioned parents who ask for my advice about their children and Olympic-sized goals. I tell them to give the following guidelines to their children:

- Focus upon the small, obtainable goals that can lead to your dream.
- Experience your sport with your mind as well as your body.
- Make what you *have* to do, what you *want* to do.

39

Make
Something
You Have
to Do
Something
You Want
to Do

CHAPTER 4

Going for the Gold
—My Own Olympic Goal

I'm not sure when the Olympics became a visible goal for me. But when it happened, I began to think of the year as a big circle. Olympic competition is always held in late summer—at a specific point on the circle. On any given day, then, I knew that the Olympics were one summer away, or two summers away. Everything I did was based upon the present as it related to the nearest Olympic summer.

I felt that I had the skills necessary to make an Olympic team, but I never went through the motions of "pumping up my ego." I hate the typical "look in the mirror and tell yourself that you're wonderful" stuff. That's not me and I don't think it works. You can't fake who you really are. You have to have a *realistic* view of what you can do and where that ability can take you. But you've got to be cautious. Plans and skills are never enough. Within every task there are elements that are simply out of your control.

I try not to worry about things I can't control, and in gymnastics that includes scoring. I've been asked how I can compete in a sport in which the judges can be so obviously subjective. And it's true. I've attended competitions such as the Pan-Am Games where out-and-out cheating even became amusing. In 1975 I traveled to Mexico City as a member of the team representing the United States in competition with countries throughout North, Central, and South America. Because of our competitive experience with other international gymnasts, the U.S. team was far superior to any others at the games. But, we barely won the team competition. And when it came time for the individual competition, the Cuban and Brazilian judges gave the Cuban gymnasts first, second, and third on almost every event. The Mexican crowds booed and the U.S. coaches protested, but we gymnasts just laughed it off as politics. Yet, the worst time that I ever felt cheated as an individual competitor occurred at the University of Nebraska. In April of 1981, while Nebraska hosted the NCAA championships, I was a member of the team representing Oklahoma University. Because of the traditionally bitter football rivalry, Oklahoma athletes don't get a very warm welcome in Lincoln. During a very basic move in my parallel bar routine I hit my leg on the bar. It was a one in a million mistake for a competitor of my experience. Just a fluke. The stands were filled with Nebraska fans and some of them began to cheer. The Oklahoma/Nebraska rivalry is always intense, but I was astonished that fans would actually cheer such an obvious mistake. I guess I just thought our sport was above the level of a street brawl. The score I got (9.35) really put my back against the wall. I knew that I would have to hustle the rest of the three-day meet if I hoped to reach the leaders.

During the final day of the all-around competition I did some of the best routines of my life—I hit everything right. I was so fired up that I was actually catching up to the leaders. The last event was the pommel horse. The horse has never been an easy event for me and so I always face it with a little bit of fear, but this day I was cooking.

The noise and confusion from the Nebraska fans flooded my senses as I stood before the horse. I quivered a bit in anxiety. I couldn't concentrate. But then I thought of all of the years of preparation and I told myself, "Just relax. Trust in your ability."

I reached up and grabbed the pommels. Just holding them gave me comfort. I felt like I was standing at the entrance of a cool, dark tunnel—ready to step in. I told myself, "Just breathe deeply, calm down, but be aggressive." My knees flexed and I jumped to enter the tunnel of concentration.

Once inside, everything was quiet—like a black hole in space with zero gravity. The tunnel was without distraction but filled with emotion. I felt nervous, yet collected—aggressive, yet at peace—unbeatable, yet unsure—confident, but afraid.

What had happened to all of the chaos and noise? I didn't worry, I just kept going. The outside world became a blur. My external perception was completely turned off and that allowed me to focus clearly and sharply on every inch of my body. I was very aware of my sense of balance as I moved with an exacting rhythm. I flowed through my routine as if I had always been meant to do this.

"Push. Stretch. Reach. That's it. Good, keep up the rhythm. Now a little quicker, good. Tight body. Perfect! Beautiful. Keep it up." All of these commands hit me in a second. I was so conscious—so aware that I could detect the slighest weakness or imbalance of any muscle and instantly correct it. It was total control.

"Okay," I told myself, "you're halfway through. Don't lose the momentum. Good. Keep tight legs and extended feet. Point—now! The end is coming, don't blow it! Concentrate!"

My arms were tired. They felt like wet concrete. "Don't worry," I said. "You can handle it. Don't second-guess, remember the rhythm, remember the practice. Don't worry about blurred vision."

Then I could see the exit from the tunnel. "That's it. Keep tight. Good. Good."

My feet touched the mat and it was over. My arms dropped to my sides in exhaustion, but even that felt good. I stepped further from the dark tunnel as I smelled my perspiration and tasted the dryness in my mouth. Once again I could feel my fingertips. My external perception returned completely. I heard the crowd and I was glad to be back. I looked to the judges for confirmation—the score was 9.8.

My friend Jim Hartung, a member of Nebraska's team, was finishing his last event, the rings. Jim has always been outstanding on the rings, and to tie me for first place in the championship, he needed a score of 9.7. He needed a 9.75 to win. I waited on the sidelines with Coach Ziert. For some odd reason Jim's routine was not right on that day; he had a "bobble" on a handstand and a big jump on the dismount. Fifteen thousand Nebraska fans went nuts waiting for the two judges to reveal their scores. The first judge raised his scorecard: 9.7. The mathematics shifted the odds as it was now all up to the second judge: if he gave the routine a 9.6, I would win, a 9.7, we would tie, a 9.8, I would lose. Jim is capable of doing a 10 on the rings, but I knew that there was no way this routine could have been as high as a 9.8. Just the deductions for the obvious errors would have brought it below that score. The second judge raised his card—9.8. All I could do was sit down as the Nebraska stands "went up for grabs." Jim and I laugh about it now, but I wasn't laughing then. I believed that I was better that day, I was coming back, I had fought hard on the one apparatus that's really scary for me, and I was so "psyched" that when I finished, I was telling myself, "You did it, you caught 'em." I knew that I should have won—but there was the 9.8 for Hartung. Who knows, maybe if the meet had been held on neutral ground, I would have received the better mark. Nevertheless, situations like that one taught me that I can't allow myself to be destroyed by factors I can't control. I can plan, and I can make things work, but, finally, there comes a time when I must emotionally give it up. Or explode.

In Los Angeles I discovered that I wanted a gold medal—I mean, I *really* wanted it, but many of the decisions regarding that goal were totally out of my hands. All I could control was my performance. All I could do was go out there and do my best. There were judges from Syria, Japan, China, New Zealand, and Great Britain and each had come with separate expectations and priorities. In addition, there were the other contestants. Maybe the Chinese would be awesome that day. Maybe no matter how perfect my performance, it might not be good enough. I knew by then that all of the factors of a victory could never be under my control.

But without a doubt the most dramatic illustration of this point occurred four years earlier when I was controlled by forces much greater than my own personal drive and goal-setting skills. I had been training hard for eleven years when, in 1980, the Russian army invaded an underdeveloped country on their southern border. As a means of demonstrating international outrage over Afghanistan, President Jimmy Carter decided that America should not go to Moscow to compete in the Olympics. I've had people ask me, "Why didn't you just go anyway?" But remember, the Olympic team is a national appointment. Individuals are not invited to compete in the Olympics; countries are.

When I first heard the rumors that President Carter was going to take the opportunity to "embarrass" the Russians, I thought it was a ridiculous idea. The Russians weren't going to be "embarrassed" by anything we did. They had invaded another country and looked like criminals to the rest of the world—if that hadn't embarrassed them, nothing would have. Besides, I thought that the Olympics were bigger than politics. I thought the whole matter would be kicked around in the news for a few weeks, people would debate, and then at the last minute we'd all jump on the plane to Moscow. I was wrong.

This was a turning point for me in another way. I was so opposed to the idea of a boycott that for the first time I made myself a public figure by speaking out in an open controversy. This made me public property and, much like a politician, I was suddenly very vulnerable to all kinds of criticism.

Moreover, I felt that those of us on the team were used by the President to soften public opinion. He created an impressive panel of athletes, called us to Washington, and announced to the press that he was going to listen to our concerns about a possible boycott and try to work out some compromise. When we got there, over one hundred athletes were put in the Gold Room and told to wait for the President. I sat on the center aisle in the third row.

A presidential aide spoke to us first. He began by discussing a plan for an "Alternative Olympics." The athletes got very restless at that point. A boycott of the *real* Olympics was yet to be confirmed by the President, and this guy was talking about an alternate. It sounded ridiculous, like we were going to go to an American city, invite all of our "friends," and then have our own "games." I was sitting next to a member of the Olympic rowing team. He turned to me and said, "What is this stuff? They've already made up their minds."

A second aide came in to set up a world map and he was followed by Zbigniew Brzezinski, the President's foreign affairs advisor. Brzezinski began talking to us about the Middle East. Actually, it was more like a geography lesson. He took out a metal pointer and began saying things like "And here's the Persian Gulf. And here's Iran." As though we were kids in school who didn't even know where Africa was. Next he began talking about the strategic importance of oil reserves in the Middle East. Anita Defrance, a member of the women's rowing team, had just graduated with a law degree from Princeton. I looked at her as she folded her arms in disgust and thought, *Maybe some of us are a little weak in foreign affairs, but surely there are others of us who know where the Persian Gulf is located.*

Thirty minutes into the meeting we still hadn't seen the President, and after the first five minutes, it was already too long. When President Carter finally entered the room, so did the press and the TV reporters. During his short speech he told us that he was going to recommend to Congress that we boycott the Moscow Games. Then he told us about other possible actions, such as withholding technology and cutting grain shipments. Toward the end of the speech he got to the real reason he had brought us there. As we had entered the Gold Room aides had placed White

House tour literature on each of the chairs, and so I copied down the President's direct quote: "I don't know which other countries will participate, but ours will not go."

". . . ours will not go." This statement came *after* we had been brought there for a discussion, and *after* he said he was going to make a *recommendation* to Congress.

After the speech, he did something that was probably very smart—he dismissed the press before accepting questions from the athletes. I'm sure the reporters would have loved to have heard the exchange. Many of the athletes had come prepared and gave some very convincing arguments against the boycott. During this time the President really talked down to us, like we were little kids. One of the guys stood and verbalized what many of us were thinking: "Our government does virtually nothing to support amateur athletics. You don't fund us. You don't sponsor us. You talk about holding back grain and technology, but you haven't done that and you *won't* do that. We have no money and no power—so you've decided to use *us* to insult the Russians."

Carter's response was absolutely pathetic. He mumbled something inaudible and the meeting was over. We were dismissed.

Before we left the room, some of the older, two- or three-time Olympians stood and suggested that we have another meeting at the Mayflower Hotel. Somebody else suggested that we should not talk to the press until we had a position statement from the group.

That was good advice because, as we walked out of the White House, we were mobbed by reporters and cameramen.

Sam Donaldson of ABC News grabbed my arm and said, "Bart. Bart. What did the President have to say?"

I tried to answer with something like, "Well, we decided not to . . ." when another athlete pulled me away and we walked down to the Mayflower.

At the hotel the meeting was in chaos. Perhaps thirty or forty percent of the athletes said that the President was right and that we should support what he was trying to do. Others screamed that the idea of a boycott was a joke and that the President was an idiot. Most were just blown away. Many just sat there, deep in their own thoughts. Some cried. Some walked out of the meeting in disgust. It was over.

Official word of the boycott came several weeks later in an announcement from Congress. I was in England, competing in the Champions All Competition. An English reporter approached me with "We've just heard that the American athletes will not be going to Moscow. Do you have a response?"

It was April, six weeks before the gymnastics trials to pick the 1980 Olympic team. Some sports had already held their trials. Some sports canceled trials at that time. But the gymnastics trials continued, partly in the hope that some miracle would happen and we would go to Moscow after all.

The boycott was sad because we were told to put aside our personal dreams for the good of a futile political maneuver. It was also sad because it acted as a precedent for further political uses of the Games. I stated that belief in 1980, and the boycott of the 1984 Olympics was further proof of political intervention.

The Olympics is one of the few events that allows the *people* of the world to come together, to share expectations and to realize similar dreams. That's a very important concept. Because even if your own country fails to win a single medal, you are still a part of a spectacular worldwide experience. You can still celebrate the Olympic ideals of sportsmanship and humanity.

After the boycott, I said to myself, "Okay, Conner, you've just got to hold together for four more summers."

The Coach's Side

Our country's 1980 boycott of the Olympic Games may have been one of the greatest tragedies that I have ever witnessed. Ironically, neither Bart nor I was excited about going to an Olympics held in Moscow. We knew that we would probably get caught in the political crossfire, but we decided that if he were as strong as possible, then any injustices would be obvious to the world. With that as our goal, going to Moscow didn't seem so bad. Bart felt that he could win either way. He could win medals, or he could win the respect of the athletes and the rest of the world. And if things did go unfairly in Moscow, people would look at him and say, "There's the guy who got ripped off. There's the guy who should have won."

Then, a few months before the Olympic trials, we heard a rumor that President Carter was considering a boycott. The media would interview Bart about the possibility and he would be appropriately serious and concerned. But privately we thought it was a joke. Boycott the Olympics? There was no way. We could not imagine how such a gesture would have had even the slightest effect upon the Soviets' national policy. The invasion of Afghanistan was a horrible event, there's no doubt about it. But we knew the Russian athletic community well enough to know that an American boycott wouldn't have fazed them in the least. They would have been *thrilled* to have awarded themselves all of the medals.

The questions came more frequently. People were discussing it in the newscasts. And suddenly it occurred to me, *The President's really serious.* It was a chilling revelation, since I simply could not see a logical cause-and-effect relationship between keeping our athletes home and giving Afghanistan back to its people. I could only conclude that this was a bluff. So I pushed it to the back of my mind and Bart's training continued in earnest. Meanwhile, I was selected to be the assistant coach for the women's Olympic gymnastic team.

The boycott didn't become a reality for me until about a week before we were to depart. Only then did I finally accept it. (A full three years later, the Russian Olympic Committee finally refunded to Bart's parents $3,500 in fees they had to advance for lodging and tickets to the 1980 Games.) It was very difficult to identify any positive route. The political issues had overwhelmed our little world as we were being told that our sacrifice was for the greater good.

Meanwhile, we were still being approached by the media for Bart's reactions. He and several other athletes were called to Washington to meet with the President. Throughout the episode Bart maintained a strong conviction that a boycott would be futile, and the public reaction to his position was sometimes hostile. I remember sitting with him during a radio talk show in Tulsa when a caller said, "How can anyone be so selfish and un-American. You must really be spoiled. Our leader, the President, decides what's best for this country. If he says we're not going to go, that's it. Stop bellyaching about it!" It enraged me that Bart would be called un-American for speaking his mind. To me, he represents the American ideal with incredible clarity and honesty. His story is as "American" as any could be.

Now, after yet another Olympics, I am not amused to see that the Russian Army still occupies Afghanistan.

The only thing that makes the whole incident palatable to me is that "fate" seems to have already been predetermined for Bart. During the final day of the '80 Olympic trials, he suffered the first of his two bicep tears. Despite the injury, he completed his routines and earned the first-place spot on the newly formed team. Had we participated in Moscow, he probably would have elected to only "patch-up" the injury— to postpone surgery until after the Olympics. There's no doubt that his athletic performance would have suffered. More importantly, to have gone to Moscow injured could have been very destructive to his whole mind and spirit.

You can make something good out of everything, look at a situation and say, "Fair or unfair, good or bad, I'm going to make the best of it." This is what we have done. This is how Bart has survived.

CHAPTER 5

My Personal Pearl Harbor
—The Setback

In 1981 I was preoccupied with several major competitions, the World Championships, the American Cup, and my responsibilities to my college gymnastics team. The Olympics seemed far away. Then suddenly, in the summer of 1982, somebody casually mentioned something about the Olympics, and it came back to me. *Good grief! It's just two summers away!* I thought.

By December of 1983 I was in top form. I had traveled to Japan to compete in a major international competition, the Chunichi Cup. The meet was essential to my preparation for the '84 Olympics.

We were in the first day of competition when it happened. I had just begun my routine on the rings when my left bicep tore away from the bone.

The bicep muscle runs along the length of the bone in your upper arm (the humerus) and is attached at the top and bottom by tendons. Upper-body strength is predominant in our sport, and a gymnast uses upper-arm muscles to gain maximum extension. Much of the control of this primary movement rests in the upper part (long head) of the bicep—the part attached to the shoulder. That's the part that takes the most abuse in gymnastics, and *that's* the part that ripped away from my bone. But a muscle is stretched like a rubber band from point to point on your bone, so when one end snaps off its anchor, the entire muscle rolls into a huge knot. It burns, as if someone has pressed a hot iron against your arm. Trust me, it hurts.

Pain is a part of any sport. It is also of two types: constructive and destructive. A gymnast, for example, is constantly adjusting and extending the movements of his body. But such adjustments can cause you to reach beyond your muscles' capacity, and sometimes that overextension results in pain. And so one movement may not feel just right or one muscle may pull a little too hard. The gymnast uses this first type of pain to direct himself toward a more proper position. It is a control mechanism in the purest sense. However, there is a second, destructive kind of pain in which continuing the activity will just cause you to further injure your body. A key skill for any athlete is the ability to tell the difference between these two types of pain. The pain of my ripped muscle was the second type and much too difficult to control. Although I did complete another strength move after the tear (a *kip* into the *"L" position*), I knew that I could never move into a *handstand* without damaging the muscle even more.

I knew this because of the 1980 tear of my right bicep. At that time I didn't know how to interpret the pain and so I completed my routine, thinking that it was just a knotted muscle. The surgery and recovery time for that injury took over a year and a half.

This time I knew better. The Olympics were several months

away. I knew that if I didn't compound the injury, it could be repaired.

Dropping out of my routine was a first for me. Never before had I just quit in the middle of a competition. We have a rule in gymnastics that if you fall off the equipment, you may continue with a one-half point deduction. All you have to do is raise your hand and signal this as your intention. You then have thirty seconds to remount the apparatus and continue your routine. So, in a reflex action, I raised my right hand to the judges. The first person to reach me was Coach Ziert. I showed him my knotted bicep and then, somewhat dazed, I walked over to the chalkbox. The truth is, I really didn't know what to do. I was trying to calm myself down—pacing around and assuring myself that everything would be okay. A part of me just wanted to sit down and cry in frustration, but another part of me had to stay in control. While pacing back and forth I told myself, "You're okay. A few years ago you tore the other arm, you had surgery, and you made it back. It'll work this time. All you have to do is go home and get it fixed." It's almost funny now—there I was in a foreign country, I didn't speak much of the language, I wasn't even sure where the airport was, but I was ready to walk on that plane that instant and get to work. Meanwhile, my coach and a couple of the other coaches were removing my handguards and leading me off the floor.

I was dazed as we crossed the arena, but one encounter really brought me back to reality. Nikolai Andrianov, the former Russian gymnast and now coach, walked up to me. This is a man whom I truly respect for what he has contributed to our sport. When he performed, the brilliance of his acrobatics ability was astonishing. He was one of my heroes. Not only that, but he had suffered many injuries himself and had, in fact, broken some age barriers by competing at a very high level until he was twenty-nine. He flicked his hand in the air as if he were batting away a fly. "Conner—too old. Los Angeles—no." My reaction to him was not one of aggression. I couldn't believe he was saying this. It almost sounded like a very bad and very clumsy joke. I didn't feel like laughing. I felt like answering, "Fine, Andrianov, that's just fine. I've just been slugged in the head with a baseball bat—go ahead and slug me again. Thank you so much."

Fortunately, another of my heroes was also nearby. Eizo Kenmotsu is a hero not only for what he contributed to gymnastics, but also for what he represents as a man. Parallel bars may be my favorite event, and on this apparatus, Kenmotsu was one of the most explosive and yet most expressive gymnasts I had ever seen. He took my hand and said, "That's okay, Bart. I'll go get some ice." Now, going to get some ice in Japan is easier said than done. Japanese trainers don't use ice with the same frequency as we do. And even in a social context, ice is considered a great luxury. Getting three cubes of ice for your Coke is difficult. Getting a bag of ice to put on an arm must be almost impossible. But ten minutes later there he was, ice in hand.

The final blow was my score. I looked to the board and the judges had posted a 1.0. Talk about salting the wound.

The Coach's Side

Three years after the '80 Olympic boycott, all of Bart's mental strength and vitality were to be given the ultimate test. The Chunichi Cup is the top international event in a country filled with elite gymnasts, and Bart was there as one of America's top contenders. Because the rings are so far above the floor, an athlete is lifted to the apparatus by his coach. After putting Bart into position, I turned to leave. I still had my back to him when I saw the crowd respond in surprise. I quickly turned and saw that he had dropped to the mat. I wanted to believe that it had been a careless fall, but the look on his face told me that he was in serious trouble. It wasn't *my* arm or *my* Olympic dream flashing before my eyes—and yet I felt his pain. I knew what the upcoming '84 Olympics meant to him and that now his participation seemed in jeopardy.

The entire year had been a series of triumphs and failures.

The World Championships had been a major success because six weeks before the injury Bart made the finals in three of six events and scored 9.9 in each. (Peter Vidmar had made the high bar finals and was the only other American who had made finals.) The previous June at the USA Championships, Bart had experienced disaster on the high bar when he slipped in a difficult move and fell to the mat. After such a roller coaster, this injury could have been the "final straw"— not only a physical disaster, but also an emotional catastrophe.

As we walked from the arena that day Coach Nikolai Andrianov, the former Russian Olympic champion, approached Bart with an incredible—an outrageous—comment. I'll never forget his face when in broken English he said, "Your arm— you tear? No more gymnastics for you. Good-bye, L.A." This was devastating to Bart. Andrianov had been a hero for so many young gymnasts of all nationalities. How he could have said such a thing to *any* kid in this situation absolutely astonished me. Remember, the Russians had not yet announced their plans to boycott the '84 Olympics, and here was a young man—one who would have been one of their greatest challenges—being led from the floor with an injury of this severity. Those of us who are coaching these athletes should be above this kind of behavior. We should be supportive of the aspirations of everyone, regardless of our personal affiliations. We're supposed to be the guides and leaders of the sport.

But I had to stay calm. My thoughts then were on finding a competent physician in Japan—someone who would not do anything that could inflame the medical situation. Also, I had to contact a therapist back in the States and get Bart to him as quickly as possible. Meanwhile, bureaucracy intruded. We had come to Japan with special tickets issued by their Sports Federation, and the officials were hedging about upgrading Bart's plane ticket from the special group rate they had obtained. They suggested he stay in Japan for the rest of the tour. At that point I remember I yelled at somebody, "Look. Here's my American Express Card. He's going home on the next available flight!" However, apart from being Bart's coach, I was also the coach of the American men's team. We had eight or nine more days left in our tour, and Peter Vidmar was in a very good position to realize *his* goals for the Chunichi meet. And so I had to put Bart on the plane alone.

I had arranged for him to be seen in Las Vegas by Keith Kleven, one of the top U.S. sports therapists. I phoned Bart's parents and, of course, his mother rushed to join him. But watching him leave like that was one of the saddest experiences of my life. I felt absolutely helpless.

The only uplifting moment of the entire incident occurred when Eizo Kenmotsu spoke his mind. Kenmotsu, who's now a judge, was an unbelievable competitor. I find most Japanese gymnasts to be very gracious, but Kenmotsu is somewhat aloof. He always gives you the impression that he doesn't really respect the present level of American gymnastics. His demeanor is even condescending at times and he makes no secret of his belief that the Japanese techniques are far superior to ours. We're just the new kids on the block, still playing around in "his sport." And so while I've certainly admired his skills, this attitude always bothered me. But upon hearing Andrianov, Kenmotsu became incredibly compassionate to Bart. He put his hand on Bart's shoulder and he said, "Maybe you need a rest now. Maybe this is a gift from the gods to give you a rest so that you may be *ready* in Los Angeles." As I look back Kenmotsu's comments seem profoundly incisive. But, of course, at that time, it was much easier to believe Andrianov!

I couldn't catch a flight for almost twenty-four hours, and by the time I got to bed the pain in my arm had stopped. In fact, my whole body seemed numb. I slept with an ice pack because I thought that would keep down the swelling and in some way help the surgeon when I got back home. I also rigged up a little sling with sweat socks to keep my arm totally immobilized. I could move it all right, I just was afraid to. It was as if I thought holding real still would keep it from getting worse.

I kept remembering the 1980 Olympic trials and my first bicep tear. There too I had been in the same inverted *iron cross* in my first routine. That time it was the bicep of my *right* arm which tore. I reached the *"L" position*—the same skill that I had reached that day in Japan, only instead of stopping, I had gone on. I finished rings and I finished five other events. I wasn't even sure the muscle was torn in 1980—I kept hoping it was just a cramp. Even so, I knew something was very, very wrong. But I pushed myself on. I knew that the boycott had been called, but what if the politics changed? What if I dropped out and the team went after all? I knew that whatever had happened to my arm, I'd probably end up in the hospital, and so I thought I might as well go out fighting. As it turned out, I was the first-place qualifier for the 1980 Olympic team, but that little bit of "bravery" cost me six weeks in a cast and months of reconditioning. I didn't have time for that now.

When I got to the terminal for Japan Airlines, I had only my razor and toothbrush and my Walkman. (Ziert lugged all of my luggage through the rest of the Japanese tour.) And for fourteen hours I was en route home: Nagoya to Tokyo, Tokyo to Los Angeles, Los Angeles to Las Vegas. On the first leg of the trip I sat in a window seat and looked out of the plane until the sun set over Mount Fuji. Soon it was dark. I didn't want to talk to anybody and so I tried to pass the time watching the Atkins lights bounce from the wing tips to a thick cloud cover. Finally, there was nothing else to do but think about my arm and my chances for the Olympics. I turned on my Walkman to make the thinking go down easier. I listened to some early Bob Dylan and then some late Rod Stewart. Halfway through the Stewart tape I found the song that I ended up playing for the rest of the trip, "Never Give Up on a Dream."

Coach Ziert had called one of our old friends, Keith Kleven.

Keith is one of the most progressive sports therapists in the United States. While at the Las Vegas Institute of Sports Medicine and Physical Therapy, he has been responsible for the recoveries of many athletes, including Larry Holmes. But just as important as his therapeutic skills was the way Keith *wanted* me to get better. There were times when I thought that he was going to *will* me back to health.

My injury occurred on Saturday and I got into Las Vegas the next day. My friend Andy Olson from Caesars Palace met me at the airport. I had become an adopted member of the Caesars Palace family since Andy, Harry Wald, president of Caesars, Terry Lanni, president of Caesars World, and Henry Gluck, chairman of the board, had taken an interest in my gymnastic career. Originally, I had been asked to participate in the Caesars Invitational Gymnastics Tournament, but later Andy had asked me to return to Las Vegas to work on fund-raisers and other public affairs events. It was through him that I became a volunteer with Jerry Lewis's Muscular Dystrophy Telethon. And almost a year before the Olympics it was Andy who had suggested to officials of Sunworld Airways that they might like to help sponsor a struggling Olympic gymnast.

Keith met us at the clinic, unlocked the building, and we walked into the lobby of his brand-new ultrasophisticated physical therapy clinic. The walls were painted with large murals depicting nationally ranked amateur and professional athletes in action. The eight-foot painting on the wall directly opposite the main entrance took my breath away. It was me—performing an iron cross on the rings.

We walked through the darkened corridors much as you would in an empty school building on a summer afternoon. It was so quiet as we passed through the inner rooms of the clinic that the snap of each light switch made me shiver. All the exercise equipment was quiet and empty—like we weren't supposed to be there. When we reviewed X rays of my arm, a radiologist focused not on my shoulder, but on my long-troubled elbow. He called it a "garbage can," worthy of any ninety-year-old man. Most obvious to him were the large bone chips "floating" in and around the joint. Actually, the bone chips had indirectly caused the bicep to rip. Because of them, my elbow had limited mobility. After a fall from the high bar years earlier, I had been unable to fully extend my arm to a straight line. Compensating for this limitation overtaxed the muscles of my upper arm.

Believe it or not, a torn muscle doesn't always *have* to be repaired. The arm will still function. It just won't function well enough for international gymnastics competition. Hold your arm out straight, twist it outward away from your body. That action is controlled by the long head of the bicep muscle, and it is an essential movement for a gymnast. If I had left the muscle unrepaired, I would never have had the strength necessary to perform gymnastics maneuvers in which this twisting must take place.

Keith immediately contacted the best shoulder/arm orthopedic surgeon he knew, Dr. Lonnie Paulos of the Latter Day Saints Hospital, Salt Lake City. The next day we were on a plane to Utah. We had actually worked backward—going first to a sports therapist and then to an orthopedic surgeon. But Keith and Dr. Paulos had earned each other's respect long ago as they rehabilitated hundreds of outstanding athletes together. My surgery was conducted at the Latter Day Saints Hospital in Salt Lake City. Three days later I was back in Keith's clinic. Dr. Paulos trusted Keith so much that I didn't return for a postoperative checkup until eight and a half weeks later.

The repair of my bicep was obviously essential, but by far the more difficult surgery was the repair of my elbow. The X rays of my joint showed massive bone chips (forty separate pieces of bone were subsequently removed). And knowing my Olympic deadline and the precision with which a gymnast's elbow must function, few surgeons would have dared to risk their own professional reputations by performing both surgical procedures at once. But Dr. Paulos was confident in his abilities and confident in my determination to execute my recovery, and so he took the chance. He "went for it."

Both my shoulder and my elbow were repaired on Wednesday,

December 7. The major surgical problem in reattaching a muscle is that you can't just "sew it back onto the bone." And so to repair my bicep, Dr. Paulos utilized a technique called the "keyhole." The upper arm bone (humerus) is a hollow tube filled with soft tissue. A small irregular hole (looking exactly like a keyhole) was drilled into the head of my humerus. Tendons are the fibers that normally attach a muscle to a bone, and so in the second step of the procedure, the tendon is knotted, pushed to the center of the bone, and pulled down into the narrow portion of the keyhole. After the knot is put in place, the bone begins to heal and the tendon is secure. The whole thing reminds me of the way a rubber band is attached to a slingshot.

That all sounds much simpler than it really is. The first and most significant problem is: Where on the tendon do you tie the knot? Also, how big should the knot be so that it won't slip out of the keyhole? If the surgeon had tied the knot in a spot that would have kept the muscle too relaxed, then I would never have been able to fully recover my strength. Or worse—had he tied the muscle too tightly, then as I exercised and performed gymnastics, I could have actually caused the muscle tissue to fray at the end and come undone. Paulos's task was complicated by the fact that my elbow would not fully extend. So he couldn't just stretch my arm out straight and measure the proper placement of the bicep on the bone. He just had to "wing it."

Keith was able to observe the four-hour surgery in progress and he told me that the last three hours were devoted to reconstructing my elbow. After most of the bone chips were out, Keith also told me that the surgical nurse became light-headed and left the operating room. Then the surgeon assisting Paulos also got ill and excused himself. It seems the work was so delicate and so near my ulnar nerve that the slightest slip could have left my arm paralyzed. There was also threat of permanent damage when the surgeon had to remove large pieces of bone from an area near another important muscle group, the triceps. One of the bone fragments actually measured over one inch in diameter.

The doctors had forgotten to tell me one little detail about the initial recovery period and so I wasn't prepared for my meeting with C.P.M. That's the cute little acronym for Continual Passive Motion, a new technique used with patients recovering from joint surgery. C.P.M. prevents two complications of such surgery: the buildup of blood (swelling) and the deterioration of the joint's ability to function normally. Swelling is especially bad after surgery of this kind and it can cause pressure and damage to muscle tissue and nerves surrounding the repaired area. When I came out of surgery, my elbow had expanded several inches from the trauma. In fact, over the next few days swelling caused my skin to become so tightly stretched that tiny blisters began to develop under the dressing. But a factor that is not always taken into consideration in surgical recovery is that when a part of the body, such as a joint, is immobilized for a long period of time, that too causes damage. The normal function of the joint is diminished and after the surgical incisions and repair work heal, the patient has to retrain nerve pathways and rebuild muscle tissue in order to make the joint work normally. And so, when I awoke in the recovery room, I was immediately aware of something lifting my sore arm up and down, up and down. The C.P.M. device consisted of a sling holding my arm, a system of cables and pulleys hanging over my bed, and a small motor. Not fun. It felt like I was doing pullups in the bed. For three days I was hooked up to that thing and it was relentless. It was even kept in motion while I tried to sleep. But I worked out a way to beat it. When left alone, I would twist my body and scoot up so that my feet were caught in a little "pullup" trapeze over the top of the bed, my body was across my pillow, and the tension from the C.P.M. machine was released just enough to give my arm a gentle little tug instead of painful pressure. But the nurses caught on. They'd check me more often and when they found me in this position, they would take hold of my feet and pull me back down into the bed.

In 1980, when my right bicep had been repaired, I was put in a large cast and kept immobilized for six weeks. The muscles in my arm, my upper back, and my shoulders simply melted away from lack of exercise and it took me months to recover my gymnastic strength.

This time we didn't have time to rebuild an entire half of my body. All of my muscles had to be kept in top condition so that when the tissue around the elbow was healed, I'd be ready to go. And so, the day after my surgery, in addition to the C.P.M., I was sitting up and exercising as much as I could. The hospital was so progressive that on the first day after surgery, they even allowed Keith to manipulate my arm with a mobilization therapy he has perfected. This is an exercise in which he moved my arm and exerted a counterpressure—a pushing against my arm—that forced me to work my muscles.

Aside from the C.P.M. and the exercise/manipulation, Keith was allowed to begin ice therapy in the hospital. This involved removing the dressing and packing my elbow in sterile ice packs for several hours a day. All four of these treatments, the C.P.M., manual manipulation, exercise, and ice, were to become the basis for my therapy back in Las Vegas.

Keith knew exactly what he was doing when he sent me to Dr. Paulos, because this was a man who treated me like a participant in the whole event. When it was time for my rehabilitation, he respected the knowledge I have of my own body, and he let me work at my own pace. This was perfect. I did not need six months in a sling. I needed a doctor who would tell me what needed to be done, establish a reasonably safe time frame in which to do it, and then send me on my way. His instructions were statements like "You can do *this* in a week, but whatever you do, don't do *that*."

My surgery took place on a Wednesday, and on the next Friday I was back in Las Vegas at Keith's clinic. It had been six days since my injury in Japan and I was ready to go. I just "barreled" right into my rehabilitation program. I couldn't move my arm very much, but I could move my legs. So, I burned the treads off the exercise bicycle, ran, and did an hour of exercises. That was all during the first morning. But even though I was mentally ready to begin, my body was still recovering from the trauma of the surgery. My mom had come over to see me, so Coach Ziert, Keith, and I took her to lunch at Caesars Palace. Midway through our meal I excused myself, went to the bathroom, and threw up my guts for fifteen minutes. After that, I attacked my exercise program with a little more caution.

> There is a characteristic common among champions—they're impatient. And when Bart was recuperating from his torn bicep, it was essential that he also cope with his impatience. Not being in the position in which he desired was very frustrating for him. It was difficult for him to accept that which he could not control. He was hurt, the Olympics were only months away, and it took a great deal of emotional stamina to hold up under those conditions. Given the same injury, almost everyone would have eventually recovered. The test here was the overwhelming pressure to recover quickly. His method for handling this emotional pressure was to combat it. He drove himself by exercising beyond all physical limitations, defying the pain and attacking therapy as if it were the enemy to be conquered. During those days my constant fear was that he would push himself too much and permanently injure his arm. This fear was also shared by both the therapist and the surgeon. After the Olympic trials, Dr. Paulos told me that he often had a nightmare in which he would see Bart lowering to a cross on the rings, causing his bicep to tear off the arm again.

The Coach's Side

The clinic looked like the exercise room in an expensive health club. Large windows. Sunlight. Bright colors of yellow, green, and blue. It was an active place, not at all like some of the hospital therapy rooms I've used. There were always dozens of people there, working on the weights and using the bicycles. These patients had so much strength and stamina, I couldn't believe it. There were recent amputees, stroke victims, people who had been maimed in automobile accidents, and one patient, Sarah, who was the sole survivor of an airplane crash. My problems seemed small compared to these. Many days they were the ones who kept me going, telling me that they were rooting for me and helping take my mind off the discomfort. The staff held aerobics classes each afternoon, and every day it was like a big party.

The focus during the first few days at the clinic was to reduce the swelling in my shoulder and elbow. When the swelling was at its worst, the diameter around my elbow was increased by three and a half inches. That much swelling caused lots of problems. First, because the tissue cells were bloated with fluid, and the spaces between the cells were bloated with fluid, there was a great deal of pressure upon the nerves in the arm. That meant pain. Second, the swelling would keep me from moving the shoulder and elbow joints.

Keith was able to reduce the swelling by carefully manipulating my arm, packing my arm in ice, and with the use of an electrical device called the Galvanic Stimulator. This machine uses a mild electrical current to drive fluid out of the tissue surrounding the surgical repair and thus reduce swelling.

One crucial aspect of Keith's long-term therapy plan was to rehabilitate my entire body. He knew that we couldn't just work on my arm and let everything else deteriorate.

Fortunately, I was able to stop the painkillers three days after my surgery. Instead, Keith developed a high nutrition program for me and supplemented it with folic acid and B complex vitamins. When the rest of my body felt better, my arm felt better.

When I had my first bicep surgery in 1980, the recovery took over a year. During that time all of my other muscle groups fell apart. When the arm had healed and I attempted to get back into the gym, I couldn't even support myself on the parallel bars without quivering with the strain. This time we couldn't allow that to happen. So I spent six hours a day—every day—at intensive physical therapy.

And so, after the first three days, my therapy pattern began to take form. Keith would outline my program to his assistant, Susie Heins, and she was my "drill sergeant." I spent the mornings stretching and using the Cybex machine to strengthen my legs and ankles. My arm could only heal and recover in a specific time span. I could work the muscles, but the tissue still needed time to heal. And so I reasoned that since I was spending that time with all of Keith's fabulous equipment, why not work to improve my weakest muscle groups. Then I could come back from all of this with a healed arm, a better elbow, *and* stronger legs and ankles.

In the afternoons I concentrated on my arm. My therapy was a combination of light movements (exercises) of the shoulder, pulling on surgical tubing (like stretching big rubber bands), more ice therapy, and working out on a series of computerized strength building machines. These things could calibrate even the slightest improvement in muscle efficiency. And, of course, when I "beat" the machine, we could readjust it to give me more of a challenge. I could set small daily goals and keep trying to beat my previous records. I knew that after working through Keith's program, I was going to be a stronger athlete in every way.

Even so, the therapy was extremely painful. I had a very strong motivation to recover and a desire to do so as quickly as possible. Knowing this, Keith was able to help me control the pain by educating me about what was going on in my body. Lots of times physical pain is actually increased because we fear being hurt. We don't understand why pain is occurring or how much pain to expect. It's like when you go into a dentist's office and are afraid simply because you don't know what's going to happen. I'll bet I came away from Keith's clinic knowing more detail about the anatomy and physiology of the human arm that anyone would ever want to know. When I understood how my joints and muscles were healing, when I understood that a specific movement was supposed to cause a specific physical reaction or pain, then I was no longer afraid. The pain became a natural element of the healing process. For example, one exercise involved gently placing weights on my arm until the elbow was fully extended. I knew that the pain I felt during that treatment was not doing harm—it was helping me. It still hurt like crazy, but I came to think of it as a "helpful" hurt. That made it more bearable.

Of all these treatments the worst was being soaked in ice. I would sit for forty or fifty minutes in this hydro-therapy room while my elbow and shoulder were resting in a large stainless steel vat filled with chipped ice. A motor swirled in the bottom of the vat and it sounded like you were stirring ice cubes in a tall glass. The rest of my body was wrapped in warm blankets, but some days that wasn't enough. I would get so cold that I couldn't stop my teeth from chattering. It felt like I was standing in a blizzard in my swimming suit. I'd put on my Walkman and crank up Rod Stewart or Bruce Springsteen.

I would never have accomplished such a recovery had Keith not taken on my case with such intensity. He was fantastic to me, not only because of his technical knowledge about physical therapy, but because of his emotional and mental commitment to me as well. I even stayed with him and his family during part of my recovery. Keith and his wife, Gaye, have a teenage daughter, Anne, and two sons, Mark and David, both in college. Staying with them turned out to be an important part of my recovery. I couldn't get homesick or feel sorry for myself when I was surrounded by such loving and caring people.

Now that it's all over, it's easy to remember the goals and the fantastic, supportive people. But there were hard times too. Twice a day, after each exercise session, I would spend ninety minutes lying on my back in a therapy room—alone—hooked up to these strange electronic machines, the Galvanic Muscle Stimulators. I'd look at this big, bloody, ugly thing that was my arm and gymnastics seemed pretty far away. I had periods when I couldn't even remember how the p-bars felt in my hands. It's like when you care a great deal for someone, but they've been gone for a while. You can't even remember what their face looks like. Sometimes in the quiet of just me and the machines I'd say to myself, "Come on, Bart. Be real. This thing may fly, but not in time."

Whenever I'd drift into one of those depressions, I would force myself to mentally execute other routines in my life. I'd visualize my bedroom at home. I would be standing there, packing my gym bag; I'd go down the steps and get into my car, drive to the gym, and walk in the back door and under the high bar on the way to my locker. Then I'd put on my warm-ups. After a while, I could see myself hitting the floor. And before long, I'd be back on track—moving through my practice routine or working out a new pattern for an old trick. This mental "practice session" would help me feel closer to a gymnastic frame of mind.

After three and a half weeks, I was ready to return to Oklahoma. The Olympic trials were six months away and during that time I would need additional therapy. I would train all week in Oklahoma, fly to Las Vegas on Saturday morning, see Keith, and then fly back on late Saturday or early Sunday.

Finally, I could return to the gym. The therapy sessions had kept me physically fit, but I hadn't been in a gym for a very long time. The calluses were gone. And I'd forgotten things like how much my ankles hurt when I take a hard landing. You can lift weights for ages, but until you support yourself on the pommel horse, you don't know gymnastics. I did my first somersault and it felt fantastic. I flipped higher than I had ever flipped before. I did a *giant* around the high bar and it felt so good that I yelled out loud. Next I ran over to my favorite, the parallel bars, and I swung up. I was so weak that I was shaking—even trembling. But man, I was up there. Keith Kleven would have died had he known how soon I was up there, but I was up. Those first few days in the gym may have been the most exciting moments I've ever spent in the sport. I was relearning, and therefore I was experiencing at an accelerated pace the same thrills that I had experienced all of those other first times. There was the first *handstand*, the first *backflip*, the first everything. Then it got to be work.

I wasn't prepared for just how *hard* it was going to be. Things which I had accomplished so effortlessly just a few months earlier seemed monumental. I'm like a lot of gymnasts in that if I want to do something spontaneous—like walk down the aisle of the grocery store and do a *round-off backflip*—then I'll do it. If I want to do a *handstand* on the Great Wall of China, I'll do that too. (In fact, I have done it.) But now, at this stage of the rehabilitation, I couldn't be so uninhibited. It was extremely frustrating. But it also was the stimulus I needed to make me work even harder.

Suddenly I realized how fortunate gymnasts are. I've always had these physical freedoms. And I've always just taken them for granted. As crazy as it sounds, this experience—the accident and the surgery—had been good for me. For all of the wrong reasons I had a chance to relive the thrill of gymnastics.

The Coach's Side

Naturally, after all he'd been through, people began to wonder if Bart had the same dream—if he dared to have it. But he did dare. I knew that he wouldn't quit. I had been Bart's coach for eight years. Once when we discussed retirement from the sport, he had said, "I'll quit only when I stop improving."

This ability to find joy in even the slightest improvement is the essence of his drive. Perhaps the best illustration of this is the way that Bart sets about to do what needs to be done. Very few people will do that. Most of us will look at a situation and immediately calculate what we ourselves will gain from involvement. "What's in it for me?" "Will this be worth my effort?" Bart, on the other hand, sees a goal and simply sets about to obtain it. You have to be very careful with people like that, because if you set them out on a mission that's meaningless, then you have wasted or destroyed so much vitality.

But the drive is not just physical. Bart is not afraid to emotionally commit himself to any project. When he tours an elementary school, he gives that audience the same energy, the same concentration, and the same drive that he does when he delivers a motivational address to a group of business executives.

I'm reminded of the incident that occurred in the first

American Cup Championships of 1976. Bart was to be the next competitor on floor exercise. As he stood on the sidelines, gathering his concentration, a little boy ran from the stands past the coaches and asked Bart for an autograph. Bart didn't hesitate as he reached down, signed the boy's program, and then shook his hand. Later when I mentioned it to him, he said, "I looked at that kid's face and I decided it was just as easy to sign his program as it was to explain why I shouldn't."

Nonetheless, this had definitely been an outrageous winter for me. On December 4 I had torn my arm. The surgery was on December 7, Pearl Harbor Day and my mother's birthday. I spent several weeks in therapy with Keith Kleven and came back to some hard rehabilitation in the gym. Then, as if I needed anything else to put in my diary, during the month of February I picked up a case of food poisoning at a fast-food restaurant and severely sprained my ankle in a *triple back* dismount off the high bar. Finally, changes in my daily eating habits got the best of me. Because of scheduling conflicts at the Oklahoma University practice gym, I had to work out from about 7:00 P.M. until 10:00 P.M. and I wouldn't eat dinner until just before going to bed. Do you remember how your mother always told you not to eat before bedtime? Well, there's a reason for that. When you lie in bed with your digestive acids churning away, they can literally eat ulcers in the bottom of your esophagus. The condition is called esophagitis and it's miserable. For three months, aside from general discomfort, I had to sleep on an incline so that my stomach acids would stay away from the affected tissue. During that time I didn't dare look over my shoulder for fear that I'd see oncoming "locusts and boils."

Everyone around Bart knew how much he cared about and loved gymnastics and how important this Olympiad was to him. And so my role during his recovery was to get him out of the gym. Many people probably thought, "What a lousy coach! The guy's trying to make it to the Olympics and his coach has scheduled a speech at the Rotary, or something." And in the spring of 1984 I literally ran Bart all over the country. But my actions were very intentional. If I had allowed him to stay in the gym as much as he wished, then he would have done too much and he would have been hurt again. And so we established a routine. He would work in the gym for a few days and then I would get him out for a day or two.

Although it may sound as if during the recovery I only knew my name and the path to the gym, I did have other activities. In 1980 I had begun doing color commentary for NBC Sports, and for years I had been involved with projects for the Special Olympics and the American Lung Association. Meanwhile, Coach Ziert and I were conducting gymnastics demonstrations for youth groups and motivational seminars for business and industry.

The next major event was to have been the American Cup in March. It was much too soon for me to have participated, but this competition had a special meaning for me. In March of 1976, I had been one of the first American Cup champions in the first big international event of the USGF. It had taken place in Madison Square Garden on my eighteenth birthday. It had also been Nadia Comaneci's first visit to this country. She had won the women's championship and I had won the men's. Talk about a thrill! The 1984 American Cup seemed like the perfect place to be *seen*. The entire gymnastics community had seen my wipe-out in Japan; they had to see me alive again. I could show them that my arm was fixed and that while I may not have been in the best shape yet, I was on my way. That was the plan. But when I got there, I was in for a shock. All of the other Olympic contenders were there in prime form. Peter Vidmar, Mitch Gaylord, and Jim Hartung looked *great. Good grief,* I thought. *I'm still a wreck.* All of this time I'd been celebrating my little flips and swings, not realizing just how far I'd fallen behind. It was the Olympic year for these guys too. They had been back in their hometowns, working out hard—every day. They were awesome and I was still slopping around. They looked sharp and crisp in every move, while I just felt lucky to hit it right one out of every three times.

I went back home and really got serious. I didn't breathe again until May. May 1984 was the time of the U.S. National Championships, and this meet was to count forty percent toward placement on the Olympic team.

It turned out to be a total disaster. I was not physically ready to compete at this level and had to scratch from the event.

Within a few months after the injury, Bart was regaining his strength and performing in small exhibitions. But it was time for him to add another dimension to his recovery— competition and performing before judges. His first post-injury meet was in mid-April of 1984 at the Emerald Cup in Eugene, Oregon. We had the permission of the officials to enter Bart in only four events: the floor exercise, pommel horse, parallel bars, and high bar. This turned out to be a real testing ground for Bart because he had looked so much better in practice than he did in the actual meet. In fact, his performances on floor, horse, and high bar were just okay, and he even fell off the parallel bars.

Three weeks later, in May, he thought he was ready to enter the National Championships in Chicago. This meet was to count forty percent toward the scores that would determine the 1984 Olympic team. (The Olympic trials, to be held in June, would make up the remaining sixty percent of each contestant's score.) I wasn't sure that Bart was ready. And I knew from our experience in 1980 that we could petition the Olympic committee to consider only his scores from the June trials. He could, in effect, have one chance at making the team, while everyone else had two.

Bart was determined to make a good showing in the Nationals, but we had agreed that if he began to falter in the meet, we would pull out and revert to the petition process. At the end of the compulsory exercise he was in second place. But unlike most international meets, in this event there was no day of rest between the first and second days of competition. And so, on the second day, Bart's strength began to falter.

He started his floor exercise, and in the second tumbling pass he put his hands on the mat—this is an automatic three- to five-tenths of a point deduction. But it was in his final tumbling run that real tragedy struck. He got "lost" in midair, underestimated his rotation, and came out of his *double back* too soon. He thought he was landing perfectly, but in reality, his center of gravity was too far forward. He bounced from his feet and literally rebounded full force onto his head. Usually when someone senses that he is about to fall like that, he will throw out his hands as an instinctual protection. But Bart was so disoriented that he didn't even do that, and so he took the full force of the fall directly on his head and neck. I still get ill when I think of how seriously he could have been injured. Thank God he was able to jump up and walk off the mat. The score was 8.65, and Bart dropped from second to seventh place.

I knew at that point that I could not allow him to finish the meet. Despite his determination, I had to take over as his coach and prevent the possibility of another fall. Furthermore, entering the June trials with low scores was actually worse than entering them on petition with no scores. And so I said to Bart, "That's it." He questioned me at first, but I honestly think he was a little relieved. Meanwhile, John Burkel (Bart's first coach and now a meet official) had told me that reporters were gathered in a side room and wanted to interview Bart regarding what could have become a major upset in the selection of the Olympic team. The story of his successes, his injury, and his attempted comeback had been in all of the papers. He couldn't just walk away from the press. So I decided to keep Bart in competition for a bit longer so that he could relax and compose himself. We knew he was out of it, but this would give him time to gather his thoughts before a confrontation with the media. He did a respectable job on his pommel horse routine, but the next event was rings—the first rings competition since Japan. I watched his turn in the three-minute warm-up and I knew he wasn't ready for a ring routine. I walked over to him and said, "Let's stop now." Bart was still hoping he could continue, and he is so determined that he would have gone through the routine no matter what. But at that point I literally took the decision away from him—I enforced my role as his coach more soundly than I had ever done before.

It is an element of any sport that when you fail, you must cope with that failure in public. John Burkel came over to us again and said, "I really hate to do this to you, Bart, but the reporters are waiting." That was one of those times when I saw Bart rise above his personal pain and meet what he saw as a responsibility. He would have rather done *anything* at that point than talk to reporters about his now-diminished chances of making the Olympic team. In the same set of circumstances many athletes would have told the press to "forget it." But without a word he stood up, grabbed his gym bag, and marched back to the press conference.

That conference could have been devastating. Think of all of the times you've seen an athlete fail and then have a television microphone thrust into his face. Think about Mary Decker at the 1984 Olympics, when, after her unbelievably tragic fall, reporters actually asked her how she felt! The last thing an athlete wants to do at a time like that is to talk about how he feels. But this press conference was different. Much to my amazement, the reporters were supportive and sensitive to Bart. I think it must have been because of all those other times when he had extended himself to them. Whatever the reason, the questions were always upbeat. I remember one in particular: "Bart, this was a disappointment, but tell us if there is another way you can still make the Olympic team." And so rather than devastating him, those reporters actually uplifted Bart. He came out of the session more determined than ever to succeed in the June trials.

After I gathered my wits, I went into a back room and spoke to the press. I knew that we had the option of petitioning the USGF to count the upcoming Olympic trials in June as one hundred percent of my efforts to qualify, and so my responses were positive.

Later, when reporters asked various people in the gymnastics community to comment about my chances of making the team, one of those contacted was Abie Grossfeld, the man who was the '84 Men's Gymnastics Team coach. His response was curt: "We don't need Bart if he's not at his best." There was no doubt that a lot of good gymnasts could have filled my spot if I had indeed been physically unable to compete. But I thought this was a low blow. I still wasn't "totally out of it"—I still had time to completely recover from my surgery. Fortunately, there were others with different opinions. I'll always be grateful to Olympian Mitch Gaylord for showing confidence in me. When he was interviewed after the Nationals, Mitch's response was flat out: "We need Bart on the team. I don't care how we do it, but we need to have him on the team."

I went back to Oklahoma, the gym, and more work.

All of my life I've had a general feeling that I am in charge of myself. When something won't work, I don't worry; I know that somehow it will be all right.

After the Nationals, I started to doubt this basic philosophy. Not every day, not even for an entire day, but once in a while I would say to myself, "You're not going to make it." I'm a positive person—but I'm not stupid. I was fighting to come back, but it was hard. People had hurt me when they'd said that I couldn't make it, and maybe I had taken their comments and turned them into "hurt" because I believed them a little myself. My body hurt. Plain and simple. That "brave little soldier" routine only takes you so far. After a while, the physical pain also contributed to the doubts. I never verbalized any of this. When someone asked how I was coming along, I'd say something like "Pretty good, pretty good" or "I'm still standin'." But the negative thoughts were pulling at me.

And one day it really got bad. I had to drive to Oklahoma City for a doctor's appointment. Like a lot of guys, my car is a source of pride for me, and on this day I had just given the Porsche a wax job. About a mile ahead I could see the highway crews doing some work. The wind kept a cloud of thick red Oklahoma dust swirling just above the road's surface. Suddenly that dust became the enemy. As I came upon it I cursed and I yelled and I slammed my hand on the steering wheel. I couldn't believe it! After all I'd been through, this stupid dust was going to mess up my car.

But when I got to that spot, the wind died down, the dust settled, and I drove right over it.

The scene was so ridiculous that I laughed out loud. I'd almost gone nuts over something as silly as dust on my car.

It was three days before the Olympic trials. I was just trying to do my best—but I was scared. Really scared. Driving along that stretch of highway I realized that tearing my bicep might have been one of the most important things that had ever happened to me. It sounds kind of crazy, but maybe I had to go through what I did in order to pull together something that had come apart in me.

Before the injury, I had taken a lot for granted. Sure I'd worked hard at gymnastics, but it was always something within my reach—something I could count on. Suddenly I wasn't so sure. Maybe I'd make the team and maybe I wouldn't. But now I knew that I really wanted it.

After the Nationals, we went back to Oklahoma for three grueling weeks of practice. This was the "emotional bottoming-out point" for Bart. Working hard, still feeling the effects of the surgery, and combating the fears that maybe he couldn't make it—this was the real test.

The trials were held in Jacksonville, Florida (the same site as the 1980 trials and the first torn bicep), and when we got to the competition, we found that we had one negative and one positive outside factor. This time the judges would only be remembering the Nationals. They would be thinking things like "Too bad, he was a great gymnast, but he's past his prime now." We wouldn't have the luxury of Bart's prior record.

But there was an additional, more positive element in the formula—Jacksonville had always been a good town for Bart. He had competed there many times before and he was, in fact, a favorite of the Jacksonville fans. This factor proved to be most significant in helping Bart make the Olympic team, for every time he walked on the floor he received resounding ovations. Most people can hang in there when everything is going well. It's the roller coaster into failure that requires perseverance and strength. In a sport like gymnastics the attitudes of others can actually accelerate the ride. If you're failing, they will usually say, "Oh, well, he's probably too old, or he's gone as far as he can go, it's sad, but it happens." Conversely, a supportive crowd can cause you to reach out for your best. Bart had heard a lot of people eager to put him down. He had been on his descending roller coaster. But the people of Jacksonville helped him come up again.

After the May Nationals, I had recognized an error in the way I had coached Bart. Making the team meant so much to him that I had allowed him to use tricks he was not ready to execute. This time I wasn't going to make that same mistake. When we planned his six optional routines, I said to him, "Let's go through the tricks step-by-step and you tell me at what points you feel somewhat unsure of yourself. What are the tricks that scare you?" When he would mention something specific, I would say, "Out it goes. Don't do it in the trials." The result was six respectable but *secure* routines.

Throughout the trials I had to constantly remind myself that making the team was Bart's only goal. I knew that no coach's pep talk would make him work any harder than he already was. And so my role became twofold: to help him maintain his confidence and to make quick and direct decisions about which tricks he should or should not do in his routine.

The first task was accomplished by removing all negative emotions or concern from our conversations. In a competition of this magnitude most coaches will keep clipboards and calculate the running scores of the top competitors. I knew that this action could be very destructive for Bart in this meet. If I had to sit there tabulating fractional differences in the scores, then he could have concluded, "We're in trouble." And yet, it was my responsibility to tell him where he stood *immediately* after his performance. There was no way that I would let him suffer through the official tabulations. He had to know instantly—was he on the team or not? And so I kept competitors' scores in my head and acted as if there were no reason to even bother keeping track.

It was also important that during the meet I give Bart short, curt modifications of his routines: "Don't do the *pike double backflip* this time" or "Put in the *layout backflip* instead." I wanted him to wear emotional blinders—to go through the routines exactly as I told him and to remove himself from any anxiety about his overall performance.

During the compulsory exercises Bart was fantastic. In the parallel bars routine he scored his first 10! And at the end of this round he was in second place.

During the first of his optional routines (the floor exercise) he slightly touched his hands down on the dismount. The score was 9.45. He had used our only margin of error and he could make no more mistakes. That would have been the perfect time for a lesser athlete to fold. But Bart didn't. He came back strong—attacked the next event, the pommel horse. Next he did a beautiful rings routine (the first optional rings performance since his bicep had torn) and an excellent vault.

It was time for his best event, the parallel bars. There is a point toward the end of this routine in which Bart does a *stutz* in preparation for his dismount. He swung through the *stutz* to the *handstand*, then his left arm momentarily faltered—buckled and gave way under his weight. My heart stopped for an instant. He couldn't afford a mistake, especially in an event in which he usually excels. Instead, he pushed his arm completely straight and held that *handstand* perfectly. He moved through his *double flip* dismount with ease and scored a 9.8. That was the turning point. He showed me the strength of his desire. I got the impression that even if the parallel bars had collapsed he would have finished the routine. In 1980, also in Jacksonville, he had been the top qualifier for that Olympic team. This time he was the last man—number six in the scores. But he had won something much, much more!

Throughout Bart's ordeal there had been people who always believed in him. As we were packing our gym bags and enjoying the victory, we were joined by one such person, Maureen Bjerke from New York. During Bart's rehabilitation she had kept in touch with him through short notes of encouragement or phone calls in which she told Bart that she knew he could do it. Maureen reached into her purse and pulled out a bottle of Dom Pérignon champagne and said, "I told Bart I'd buy him this when he made the Olympic team."

Now everything I did, every routine in every competition and every practice exercise, was geared toward bringing me to my very best in August of 1984. I couldn't be at my peak in September. It *had* to be August. Every day prior to the Olympics I would review those specific factors that could make me feel and be my best in August. It can get to be something of an obsession. Usually I am not superstitious, but my injury caused me to take on some of the habits for which athletes are notorious. I'd remember something insignificant that I'd done during the trials of the '76 and '80 Olympics—maybe I'd always worn a yellow shirt on Tuesdays; whatever it was, it had worked—so I thought that I'd better do it again. The closer we got to the Olympics, the crazier these things became. I'd go to a reception in June and say to myself, "Better not eat the chili tonight, because you might regret it in August." And, of course, as the time drew closer, the anxieties grew more out of proportion. If I got a hangnail, I'd wonder if it could affect my Olympic performance.

Joan Benoit, gold medalist in the marathon, told me that for months she postponed knee surgery for fear that "fooling around with it" would in some way harm another part of her running form. She endured the pain rather than risk the parts of her body that were functioning perfectly. It's irrational, but that's what happens when you're superstitious.

Sometimes pre-Olympics anxiety can become outrageous. When I met Mary Decker, she wasn't like any champion that I had ever known. She was depressed and paranoid about almost everything. She'd say things like "I can't wait for this to be over!" or "My legs hurt, my hair looks terrible, and my car won't work." And yet, she is one of the greatest women runners alive.

These stories seem silly now—a yellow shirt wouldn't have helped my performance and Mary Decker looked great despite what she thought of her hair—but they illustrate how each of us handles the premeet tension. No Olympic athlete was a *superhuman machine.* We were all just hardworking people trying to emotionally hold ourselves together so that we could do what we had dreamed to do. More importantly, this kind of tension is a vital motivator. Two years before the Olympics I knew that the team finals would begin for me on a Tuesday—July 31, 1984. I knew what the gym would probably look like. I knew what

I would wear. What I would feel. How I would walk into that arena. And I played that scene over in my mind a million times. Mental rehearsal is essential for any action requiring physical control, so I would envision my trial routines as if I were a judge, outside of my own body. And I would envision them as if I were actually living the experience. Even the timing would be the same. I'd imagine chalking up my hands the exact number of seconds that I do in every practice. It was always as real as I could make it. I was ready.

CHAPTER 6

More Than Gold
—Los Angeles, 1984

When most people think of an Olympic training camp, they envision something like a Boy Scout overnight with tents, curfews, and restricted meals. The training camp for the U.S. Men's Gymnastics Team was a Holiday Inn on Wilshire Boulevard and a gym on the campus of UCLA. There we were, training for the most important athletic event of our lives and staying in Westwood, the hottest little community in Los Angeles.

The camp was actually divided into two segments. The first ran from June 17 to June 25 and the second was from July 8 until July 14.

Each morning during the first camp we would drive to a gym on the University of California at Los Angeles campus, spend an hour doing calisthenics or stretching exercises, get a massage or physical therapy, return to the hotel, relax, and have lunch. We went back to the gym at two o'clock each afternoon and worked out until about six. During these workouts the coaches identified and helped us with our weakest skills. So instead of performing entire routines, we did the same move over and over each day.

It wasn't the kind of strenuous schedule that most people would imagine. And it left a lot of time for us to explore Los Angeles. Nissan Datsun was the official sponsor of the Olympic Gymnastic team, so when we got to town, the local dealer gave us the use of ten white '84 Datsuns. There we all were, buzzing around Westwood in those neat little cars. Tim Daggett really knocked us out one day. He came into the hotel, all excited about his newfound fame as an Olympic gymnast.

"You guys won't believe this—everywhere I go people pull up alongside of me to honk and wave and wish me good luck in the Olympics."

You've got to imagine what this guy looks like—he's enormous, with broad muscular shoulders and arms—sitting in this little white Datsun.

So I said, "Daggett, what's the matter with you? First, you *look* like you just escaped from a gym, and second, you've got a three-foot sign on the side of the car that says 'Official Car of the U.S. Olympic Gymnastics Team'!"

He said, "Oh, yeah. I guess you're right."

We were quite a diverse group, although we all seemed to come from the same neighborhoods. Mitch Gaylord, Peter Vidmar, and Tim Daggett were students at UCLA. Jim Hartung, Scott Johnson, and our alternate, Jim Mikus, all trained at the University of Nebraska. I was from Oklahoma University. Actually, these affiliations had more to do with the physical locations of our coaches than it did with our hometowns. We were from all over the country and we had traveled all over the world. Each of us had competed against one another in American events and had been teammates in international competition. Gymnastics at this level is a very small community.

Each gymnast brought with him a set of unique strengths. Mitch Gaylord, for example, was called the "trickster" because of his wild explosive routines. He would come into a gym and immediately begin playing on the high bar. The dynamic manner in which he performed his sensational moves really made you take notice. Despite all of this explosive gymnastic personality, he may have been the most shy member of the Olympic team.

When I first knew him, Mitch would spend an hour and a half in the gym and then head out to the beach. Eventually, he got smart and started taking his training and his work schedule seriously. Before, he had been somewhat of a rebel, but finally he saw the benefit of a little extra work and a little more concentration. Mitch was also the only team member to live away from the rest of us. (Family friends had asked him to look after their house in Bel-Air.) He's very introspective, keeping to himself a lot, and, I think, more than anyone, Mitch may have needed to be alone during the weeks before the Olympics. The pressure for him to succeed was enormous.

I first met Peter Vidmar in the 1978 USGF Nationals. Ironically, that meet was also held in the UCLA Pauley Pavilion. Kurt Thomas took first place that time, and I took second. After the finals, kids were coming up, asking for advice and for my autograph, and I noticed this guy standing off to the side. It was Peter, still in his uniform. He waited quietly and didn't say anything. Finally, when the spectators had gone, he walked up to me, introduced himself, and said something about being happy to have competed with me. This gentle and unassuming quality is a strong part of his character. But once he gets to know you, he turns out to be quite a comedian. (He's especially good at mimicking famous people.) He's only been married a year and for the next twenty or thirty years people will probably still tease Donna and Peter about how they spent their honeymoon working at a gymnastics training camp. More than any of the other members of the team, Peter's style of gymnastics reminds me of my own approach to the sport. He doesn't always do the most difficult tricks in a routine, but he tries to perform perfectly and to link the skills together in a creative or artistic manner. I would say that he is a neat, clean gymnast.

To my knowledge, Scott Johnson was the only one of us who did not come through the normal gymnastic channels of the USGF Junior Development and Age Group programs. Rather, his early years were spent in the Colorado Springs school system. Scott's incredible strength gave him an ability to quickly learn tricks. But the fact that he did not come through the Junior Development program put him at a great disadvantage when he went against more elite gymnasts. The first time I saw Scott was in the 1980 U.S.A. Championships. In that meet he scored something like 9.6 on every apparatus except the horse. And on the horse he scored around a 7.6. He solved the problem by going to Nebraska to work with Jim Hartung, an expert on the pommel horse. Jim and I knew immediately that Scott was good—all he needed was a little specialized attention. In Columbus he ranked about twentieth, and the next year he was fourth. Every time I see Scott work I see improvement. I can't believe how his strength makes an event like the rings seem so effortless.

Tim Daggett is "The Bull." He and Scott were the youngest members of the team, and as with Scott, the rest of us "old hands" were soon to pick out Daggett as a real champion. He was a part of the Junior Development Program (sponsored by the USGF) just when the Russians were astonishing the world with explosive, dynamic tricks. And so Tim and kids like him were encouraged to push themselves to their physical limits. Coupling that philosophy with his natural strength and drive means that Tim literally hurls himself into everything. He has dislocated his ankles, he has had a couple of operations, and he has wiped out on every piece of equipment. But he still does everything full blast. He doesn't work an apparatus, he attacks it. When you watch Tim on the horse, you would swear that he could rip the pommels right off the thing. The rest of us kid around that if he doesn't kill himself, Tim could be one of the world's greatest gymnasts.

Jim Hartung started gymnastics when he was five years old. And by the time the rest of him caught up to his ears, he was one of the most fantastic tumblers I've ever seen. Tumbling has definitely been the stabilizing factor of Jim's abilities. Because of this special skill at acrobatics, his dismounts were consistently the best of anyone on the team. A key to this skill is something we call "air sense"—a natural ability to remain oriented when you're flipping through the air. The hardest part of tumbling is knowing where the ground is. To illustrate this point you can lean your head back, keep your eyes open, and shake your head as hard as you can. What you will see is what the gymnast sees in a twisting flip. And some people, while flipping through the air and seeing this blur, simply cannot find the ground. But Hartung is like a cat, he always knows which way is *down* and he always lands on his feet. I think that because he began at such an early age, he has no *fear* of tumbling. Lots of kids have bad falls that make them afraid to relax in the air, but not Hartung. It's like second nature to him now.

To the outside world we probably seemed to be all alike, but actually, every member of the team was an individualist with diverse talents and skills. The man in charge of bringing all of this diversity together into a team was Abie Grossfeld, head coach for Southern Connecticut State University in New Haven. As a two-time Olympian, he literally knows everyone in the sport—primarily because everyone else makes it a point to know him. Since the team was made up of factions from UCLA, Nebraska, and Oklahoma, Grossfeld was a "highly respected neutral party" and, thus, the perfect political choice for the role. He was the perfect choice in another way as well. The '84 Olympic Team was a team of very strong individual competitors. All of us had considerable experience as well as national and international success. In addition, we all had individual training schedules. Abie's personality and coaching style allowed that individuality to flourish. He didn't walk around the gym shouting orders and directions. Rather, he would give us each an individual workout schedule and then expect us to be responsible for our own actions.

Abie was always there for support and advice, but he didn't treat us like beginners. For example, Tim might have decided that he needed to spend an hour each day on the pommel horse, while someone else might have elected to spend twenty minutes on it. We all knew what we needed to do to get ready, and Abie allowed that to happen. He was also right there if we tried to "slop around" in any event. I might slide through a ring routine, for example, and then decide to go on to vaulting. Abie was always there, seeing everything, and before long he would come over to me and say, "Bart, that ring routine was pretty good, but I'd like to see it again."

As an example, Abie worked for many days with Mitch Gaylord on the spectacular high bar trick, the *Gaylord II*. Some days Mitch didn't want to do it because it's scary, and difficult, and you can wipe out pretty badly. When that would happen, Abie would say something like "It really would be nice if you'd catch that trick three or four times today."

Abie preferred the dynamic, explosive approach to gymnastic performance—he wanted us to bounce off the ceiling and leave the crowd gasping in astonishment. Li Ning of China does *triple flips* and *double twisting double backflips*—spectacular moves. And to Abie, that's gymnastics. This interest in the skill level of individual tricks actually helped me. It encouraged me to blend more acrobatic skills into my artistic expression.

The first time Abie and I had a serious disagreement, I think that I gained his respect. It was in 1982 and we were together in Volklingen, Germany, for a preliminary competition before the World Cup in Zagreb, Yugoslavia. The U.S. team consisted of three athletes: Hartung, Vidmar, and me. Abie was our coach.

The most significant point at which team goals can conflict with individual goals is the lineup, the order of competition. Psychology determines patterns that are most advantageous to a team effort. And to understand the patterns, you must realize that judges are people first and judges second. This means that they tend to be conservative on the first few scores so that they can have room to maneuver if later routines are significantly better. After all, if the judges gave the first competitor a 10, what would they do if his performance turned out to be the weakest of the

My Baby.

High School State Meet.
My first score over 9.0!

Pretty slick! Age fourteen.

Whew — I made it!

My first giant swing —
first torn callous too!
I was ten, then.

The fellas! Scott, Jim and me.

Mitch — nice glasses!

Summer workouts '77.

Gone fishin'.

With Carol and Carl Lewis on the Olympic bus.

Doesn't everyone have a pommel horse in the basement?

1980 boycott was a disappointment for all of us...

To Bart Conner
With best wishes,

Nancy Reagan   Ronald Reagan

But 1984 made up for it.
Everyone seemed happy!

"Oh say can you see..."

V-seat overlay — now I'll do it with my eyes shut!

neat, huh?

Paul's Valley...
I wanted the car, all they
gave me was the sign.

Isn't this how you're supposed to do it?

Yes, it's real gold!

Our YMCA team —
Tim Slottow got the trophies.
I got a new sweater.

Isn't this fun? Pam, Tim, Julyanne, Tracee, Mitch,
Jim, Peter, Mary Lou, me, Marie, Scott, and James.

The dynamic duo—
me and Tim Slottow

What a bruiser! Age twelve.

Michael (in background) liked the tree house—
I was too busy.

Could this be the start of something?   My first medals: Coach Borkel,
                                        Bruce and me.

Thanks for holding down
the horse, Dad (on left)

Help, Coach! I'm stuck!

Conner spin.

Everyone's got to do one picture like this!

Planche

Scissors

Some competition memories...

V-seat

Floor exercise

so now what should I do?

event? Because of this, a good team strategy is to put a guy in that first spot who will go out there and "knock out" the judges. If he can cause the judges to score high, then each subsequent competitor will get a relatively higher score. If you follow a good performance, you don't even have to be better to receive a higher score. In the Olympics, I was usually third or fourth in the lineup. If I did well and got a 9.8 or a 9.9, then the last two or three guys were in a better position to receive higher scores. To illustrate the point even further, let's say that a guy at the end of the lineup missed a small part of his routine. The judges would look at the other scores, look at the past reputation and performances of the athlete, decide that he was usually a 9.9 performer, but this time they would give him a 9.8. Had that same guy gone up early in the lineup and had he performed exactly that same routine, he might have only scored a 9.7 or 9.6. His very position in the lineup sets the point of reference for the judging. It may not make sense at first, but it's human nature. And in gymnastics all evaluations are the result of the nuances of human nature. Believe me, it's enough to drive you absolutely *nuts*.

All of this jockeying around and trying to "outpsych" the judges had but one goal—adding up respectable team points. It's difficult for team members to forget what will be best for them as individuals—after all, everybody wants to be the guy at the end of the line. Instead, they must think of what is best for the team.

Sometimes this means that individual opportunities are lost. Since the judges aren't expecting a 9.9 or a 10 from the first guy out, he literally sacrifices most chances to win an individual medal. The lineup, therefore, is rightfully a coaching decision. There's no way six team members can come together and vote on who's going to run out there first as a sort of sacrificial lamb.

Before the '82 meet in Germany, Abie had pulled us all together and had begun in his usual manner, "Now, I want you guys to know that the most difficult job for me is picking the lineup." He then told us that Hartung was to be up last three times, Vidmar was to be up last twice, and I was to be up last once. This wasn't fair. Hartung, Vidmar, and I were evenly matched—no one of us should have been the sacrificial lamb more than any of the others. The fair way would have been for each of us to be first in the lineup for two events, second for two events, and last in the lineup for two events. After Abie told us his plan, we were silent. We each knew how things stood and we each knew the lineup wasn't fair. After the meeting, I went to Abie's room. I surprised myself and spoke up. "Abie, this is bull. I can't believe that we have three gymnasts of equal ability and you're trying to decide which minuscule factor may mean that one guy should go up last. Why not let us split up the spots in the lineup? You know that on a given day, any one of us could go out there and win any single event. Nobody can predict which one of us will hit—so why not give us all a fair chance?"

Abie was astonished. He couldn't believe that good ol' Bart—the guy who always did everything he was told—would actually confront him. But he treated me with more respect after that, and I'm glad I said what I thought was right.

After our initial Olympic training camp, we each went home and worked in our own gyms, planning to return to L.A. and our second training camp on July 8.

We came back to L.A. before the Olympic Village opened, and so everybody but Mitch stayed back in the Holiday Inn on Wilshire. We started the camp with an even pace—about four or five hours a day. But, of course, our practice grew more intense. We worked through complete routines, trying for as much competitive energy as we could muster. Nobody was slopping through his workouts now. Everyone knew very well what the Olympics meant to all of us. After the workouts, we were all pretty exhausted. We'd drive from the gym to a 7-Eleven store on Westwood Boulevard, load up on Doritos and beer, take it all back to the hotel, and sit in the Jacuzzi for an hour. (Not exactly what you'd expect from world-class athletes.)

One day we decided that we needed to get away from it all or go nuts, so the whole team drove out to the Santa Monica Pier. The man running the bumper cars recognized us, and since nobody else was there, he let us ride for about an hour—at no charge.

What a riot! As if it would have surprised anyone, we all turned out to be pretty aggressive drivers! (Fortunately, I had taken the Bondurant driving course a couple of years before, so I had a little advantage.) Later we walked along the arcade, pitched baseballs at milk bottles, and finally ended up on the beach, where an old wino recognized our warm-up suits and asked if we could get him some tickets to the Olympics. Yeah, right!

On July 14 we were one of the first American teams to move into the Olympic Village. Some of the others didn't arrive until a week later. The official team processing took place at the Marriott Hotel near Los Angeles International Airport. That scene was a cross between a traveling circus and registration day on the campus of a Big-Ten university. Everybody was trying to read the signs and the maps, trying to figure out where to go. Once inside the hotel, we picked up our "official Olympic garb." Levi's had provided all of the U.S. team clothing, so our first stop was through that station. It looked like what you see in an old film about army boot camp, except everything was red, white, and blue instead of army green—a long line, outstretched arms, and stacks of clothing: warm-ups, coats, ties, dress pants, shirts, belts, shoes, clothes we were to wear in the opening ceremonies, and sports uniforms. We were measured and the clothes were altered and delivered to us in about two days. In addition to all of our clothing, we and the foreign athletes also received articles from every official Olympic sponsor. They gave us each a large red, white, and blue Olympic gym bag and we filled it up with a scrapbook made out of denim, Olympic team pins, and a second, smaller gym bag filled with official toothpaste, Fuji film, Visine, M&M's, Snickers, Right Guard—every product that was a part of the Olympic sponsoring network. It was just like Christmas. We were totally engulfed in official Olympic products—self-sufficient. United Airlines even had a special desk where an athlete could ship back stuff he had brought from home and really didn't need.

Of course, we were very much aware at this time of the foreign teams that would not be there.

The last day of my eight-year college career was in April of 1984. I was driving home from a final in Journalism Law. I turned onto my street and in my driveway was a Minicam van from station KWTV, Oklahoma City. I thought to myself, *Isn't that great. They've heard that I've finally finished college.*

I jumped out of my car, walked across the lawn, and met the reporter. She put a microphone to my face and said, "We're live in thirty seconds. What is your reaction to the Russian boycott of the Olympics?"

My first words were not exactly prophetic: "I don't believe it. The Russians spend too much money on amateur athletics and they link their successes in sports too closely to their political reputation. It'll never happen." (So far I'm zero for two in predicting Olympic boycotts.)

When I got into the house, the phone was ringing as everybody from the *New York Times* to the *Los Angeles Times* was calling for interviews. I spent the afternoon floating on a raft in the middle of the swimming pool—an iced tea in one hand and the portable phone in the other—talking to reporters and answering questions on live radio call-in shows all over the country. I thought, *If I'm gonna have to spend six hours on the phone, I might as well enjoy myself. At least I'll get a tan out of this thing.*

But back to the Olympics. After team registration, we jumped onto "official Olympic buses" and headed out to the village. When we pulled onto the USC campus, past the three barbed-wire fences, the guards, the machine guns, and the first security checkpoint, somebody in the bus said, "Well—there are the guns—this must be the Olympics." But none of the security precautions seemed strange to me. I've been to a lot of international competitions and security is the same at all of them. You get used to seeing guys standing around with machine guns.

The dormitories in the village had been arranged to house groups of six or seven athletes in two-bedroom apartments. When we hit the door of our apartment, everybody wandered around looking the place over, but I had been on the road enough times to know what to do first—I checked out the beds. There were two sets of bunks in one bedroom, and one set of bunks and a single bed in the second. Never one to be shy about grabbing the best spot, I threw my bags on the single bed and thus declared my territory as senior man. Peter and Tim bunked in the room with me, while Hartung, Mitch, Scott, and Jim Mikus took the second bedroom. Mitch only stayed with us for a couple of days, however. He's always had a problem with claustrophobia, and four guys in a room was more than he could handle. Peter often left to stay with his wife, so usually there were just five of us in the apartment. Even then it was still cramped. One night about three days into the session, Scott ripped apart one of the bunks and carried his bed into the dining room for a little extra space.

The rest of our tenth-floor apartment consisted of a bathroom, a dining area, and a living room. On that first day, I opened the curtains in the living room to check out the view. To my left I could see the roof of the next building. A couple of S.W.A.T. cops were standing in the sun with their black uniforms, binoculars, caps, and flak jackets. One of them rested the butt of an automatic weapon on his hip and used his other hand to shield his eyes from the glare. They looked like extras in a Clint Eastwood movie, but we were all glad they were there. Security was an integral part of the village. Every once in a while some athlete would accidentally lean on a fence and set off the alarms. At that time the security guards would come running, but primarily the police blended into the background. That is, except for the beach umbrellas. As we walked through the village we couldn't help notice all of the bright white beach umbrellas on every rooftop. We'd look up to those roofs and half expect to see girls sunbathing. Then a S.W.A.T. man would come out from behind the umbrella and we'd be back to reality.

Our apartment overlooked the Olympic pool and diving well. In fact, our windows were directly across from the diving platforms. After seeing how close we were, we even joked about setting up bleachers and selling tickets during the diving competition. The pool had been donated to the Olympics by McDonald's Corporation, and I think it was Peter who first started calling it "McPool."

Anytime you put people together in such unusual circumstances, you're bound to create some interesting interpersonal dynamics. I'd bunked with these guys on countless road trips, but nothing had prepared me for rooming with Tim Daggett! "The Bull" has a very healthy, but very disarming, way of releasing his premeet tension. He has nightmares. Loud ones. Our beds were separated by a space of less than three feet, and once at about 3:00 A.M. Tim reached over in his sleep and grabbed my shoulder. I turned to look at him and he literally yelled into my face, "Bart. Bart. The guys are here so we can go ahead and move this stuff now!" Then he calmly climbed back into his bunk. Needless to say, I was awake the rest of the night. When I told him about it the next day, we all had a good laugh, as everybody else had his own "Daggett nightmare" story.

With the swimmers doing laps in the pool in the early morning and Daggett at night, it's a wonder we got any sleep at all.

Throughout the Olympics I spent most of my working and free time with Jim Hartung. We had shared the hard times and the fears, and now we wanted to share the sheer pleasure of just being in the Olympic Games. We were very relaxed during the competition because we both felt that our success had already happened. We were at the Olympics, and for us, *that* was the ultimate experience. Once we were talking about some of the top Olympians in other sports—the stars—and how tense they were getting. Some of them had already hired lawyers, agents, publicists, and theatrical managers who were sitting in the wings, saying, "Win your gold medal and then we'll really *go to town*." What pressure! There was no way that those guys could just enjoy being there.

If you would take any large college campus, add a few extras like an open-air bistro, hang colored banners from all the lampposts, and encircle the whole place with three stages of electrified barbed wire, then you would have the Olympic Village. In the evening lots of athletes would put on old warm-ups and roam throughout the commons area, jog, sit on the grass, or get food at one of the snack bars. The conversations were usually pretty surface: "Hi, how are things going with your training?" "Are you

nd Wisconsin
g Ten Defeat

Phone
-1240

scoring was on
Todd Gregoire
Emery raced
ne yard in the
ur yards in the

played well,"

finished with
ies to lead all

ed we can put
board," Emery
as been down,
k."

g junior Mike
ack, converted
es in the first
0 for 225 yards.

"Keyes came on and played a l
better in the second half," McCla
said. "I never thought about benc
ing him. I wanted to give him
complete opportunity to get the e
perience."

Keyes, a sophomore, said th
Badgers "knew we had to score
the second half to be in the gam
and we did what we had to do."

"I seemed to get more conf
dence with every series I played,
he said.

Keyes put the final touchdown o
the board when he found Brian Bo
ner with an 11-yard scoring pass i
the closing minute of the game.

Wide receiver Tim Fullingto
caught six Keyes passes for 1
yards.

edar Grove Capture
yball Regional Titles

e Conference
pion Ozaukee
an Falls Class
rence runner-
the Hustisford
day.
e to sectional
sites yet to be

nal involving
as, Sevastopol
ilbert.
s unbeaten so
ed back host

Brillion also advanced to th
final with a win over Random Lak
which beat Chilton in its openin
match.

The Warriors dropped the firs
game of the final, 15-10, but the
came roaring back with successiv
15-5 victories and the champior
ship.

Tammy Wolff led the Warrior
with a perfect 40-for-40 serving ac
curacy, while Beth Wickland had a
outstanding tournament in the hi
ting category, according to Ozauke

the food?"—stuff like that. Then the
ple and the conversation would
training going?" The unspoken
see you, but I have someplace to
o do. Once in a while you might
to hustle girls, but most people

articularly strange at night. While
u could hear loud music coming
o," Studio '84.

t for many of the athletes. Once
ld friend, Lavinia Agache. Lavinia
o was a member of the Romanian
en Nadia Comaneci toured the
o idea how old she is because the
lency to lie about the ages of their
er with the team we were told she
teen. Two years later I saw her in
at she was fourteen. It's a standard
n, East German, or Russian girl how
oach for the answer.

kidded around when we've met in
tarted at a meet in Milan when I saw
cking cap bigger than her head. On
pulled it down over her face. After
e would punch me or steal my gym
ked up a little English, she said to
an only guess that they show Amer-
ut regardless, her "Tom and Jerry"
ke.

ed into joggers. Night was when the
came out to drop a little weight.
d warm-ups and huff and puff around
whales. The only thing you had to
s getting in their way.

lifters had to work hard when you saw

Charge it!! Lifestyles Departmer
$50. Four-piece hostess set, Re
o s/knife; one butter knife; a
l salad forks; dinner knives, dinner
ns; 8 each: dinner knives, dinner

what they ate during the day. I remember going into a cafeteria line and watching one of those guys fill up his tray with three steaks, french fries, two glasses of milk, a chef's salad, and a dish of carrots. As a last thought before walking to his table, he stuck a loaf of French bread under his arm.

The formal opening ceremonies began on July 28 and it was hot and sunny, just as you would imagine Southern California in the summer. And the heat added to the excitement. Athletes from each country entered in alphabetical order with the host country coming in last. While awaiting our turns to enter, we stood in the adjacent L.A. Sports Arena. The Olympic Committee had been very thoughtful and arranged a series of huge closed-circuit television screens so that we could watch along with the rest of the world, but the whole system malfunctioned and we had no picture. So when we walked through the tunnel connecting the two facilities and finally entered the Coliseum, I really wasn't prepared for the energy and strength in that crowd. It was overwhelming. I had been present at the 1976 Olympics, but to be in the Olympics when they are being held in your own country is like no other experience. I had read that over two billion people were expected to see the worldwide Olympic TV coverage. Unbelievable!

The moment I stepped onto that field, the Olympics were a triumph for me. As far as I was concerned, this was just the icing on the cake. I was here. I had made it. I had absolutely *nothing* to lose.

I marched into the Coliseum next to Jim. We were really "psyched"—waving to all of the people, laughing, and getting goose bumps. All we could see were thousands and thousands of smiles and flags. And I think that everybody in the stands marched every step right along with us. A few months after the Olympics, I got a letter from a young girl who said, "Did you see me that day in the Los Angeles Coliseum? I was the one smiling and waving the flag." And do you know what? I did. If only for an instant, I actually did feel and "see" every single face.

Then, as we moved around the track, the funniest thing happened. I said to Jim, "Wouldn't it be great to spot somebody you knew in this mob?" No sooner were my words out when he said, "Bart, look. There's your mom." Sure enough, I could see my mom and dad just past the stairs where Rafer Johnson ran up to light the torch and eight rows up from the track. Right there, with almost one hundred thousand people, I saw my parents. Seeing them reminded me that I wasn't alone. My being there represented the accomplishments of a lot of other people.

After the ceremonies, every one of those hundred thousand people hit the parking lots and sidewalks surrounding the Coliseum. It was two hours before we made it to the village. Now it was time to get back to reality—and prepare to compete.

The village was about fourteen miles from Pauley Pavilion (our competition site) so we spent a good deal of our day on the Santa Monica Freeway. Our morning routine consisted of stretching exercises in a gym at USC, followed by a light workout and massage from the trainers. We would wait for competition by relaxing in our rooms. Most of the guys spent the time playing Trivial Pursuit. (Vidmar was declared unofficial champion.) Thank God gymnastics was up early in the schedule, because after the opening excitement, the tension of competition returned.

Many Americans are still unsure of the rules of gymnastics competition, but the parameters of the sport are relatively straightforward. Major events such as the Olympics consist of three competitive phases: All-Around Team Competition, All-Around Individual Competition, and Individual Apparatus Competition.

Men's gymnastic competition consists of six events: floor exercise, pommel horse, rings, vault, parallel bars, and high bar.

Team competition requires all six team members to perform two routines in each of the six events. This includes a compulsory routine in which the gymnast performs a prescribed set of skills and an optional routine in which the athlete designs his own program. Each team throws out the lowest score on each apparatus and thus applies only the five best individual scores to the final team score. Thus, thirty compulsory scores and thirty optional scores make up the final team score.

After the team compulsories and optionals, the top thirty-six scorers, with a limit of three from any one country, are allowed to compete in a second round called the All-Around Individual. After winning the gold medal for the team competition, Peter Vidmar, Mitch Gaylord, and I reached this phase of the competition. Along with the three top performers from the other countries, we each did another round of the six events. Our scores from the team competition and this all-around competition were compiled to select the best all-around gymnast. This gold medal was awarded to Koji Gushiken from Japan.

The second individual medal competition is the Individual Apparatus Finals. After the team competitions, the top eight scorers on each apparatus (with a limit of two from a single country) are then allowed to compete in still another routine on that piece of equipment. I was in the individual finals of both the floor exercise and the parallel bars, and it was on the bars that I earned my second gold medal.

The competition schedule was:

Sunday, July 29	Men's Team Compulsory Exercises
Monday, July 30	Women's Team Compulsory Exercises
Tuesday, July 31	Men's Team Optional Exercises
Wednesday, August 1	Women's Team Optional Exercises
Thursday, August 2	Men's Individual All-Around
Friday, August 3	Women's Individual All-Around
Saturday, August 4	Men's Apparatus Finals
Sunday, August 5	Women's Apparatus Finals

When he began the '84 Olympics, Bart's arm was still mending. The scars on his shoulder were purple and tender. In order to straighten his elbow to a full extension, he had to use ice, whirlpools, and lots of aspirin. More importantly, he hadn't had an opportunity to experience many competitive situations yet, so his self-confidence was not fully rehabilitated. An athlete, particularly a gymnast, must have the daring, or just plain guts, to repeatedly confront the physical risk necessary to complete a routine. There is a moment as he does something like a *double somersault* or a release move on the high bar when he must have tremendous courage and confidence in his own abilities. A severe injury destroys that. And it takes many recurrences of a successful performance under pressure before that confidence will have healed as much as the body.

The planning, the creativity, and the preparation were over. Individual coaches were not to participate in the Olympics, so I thought that I would just become a supportive bystander. That didn't prove to be the case.

Walking into Pauley Pavilion on the first day of competition was some kind of *fantastic* thrill. I had imagined the scene so many times as a part of my mental training: marching in with my gym bag, the lights and the crowd, surrounded by the other team members, the coaches, and managers. Now here it was in "real life." I've been competing for so long that I don't get really nervous. Now I just get anxious. But this was the Olympics—this was different. Part of me couldn't even believe that I was really there.

Yet, in the midst of all this excitement, something was terribly wrong. This was supposed to have been the greatest day of my life and I felt awful! I felt so lethargic—like I had molasses for blood, or something. This was not like me at all. Usually on the day of any competition I am really "cranked up," running around the mats and anxious to get something on the scoreboard. Not today.

I decided to fight it and really threw myself into my warm-up. But as I was running down the vaulting runway, my legs were heavy and my body was awkward. I didn't feel sharp. I couldn't believe it. I thought, *This is unreal! After all that's happened this past year—here it is, the Olympic Games—and you feel crummy! How can you let yourself feel crummy?* For the previous week I had been tapering down, just like I was supposed to. I had been eating well. I had been sleeping well. I had been doing all that I could that was right, and yet I felt so rotten.

The order of events is selected by a premeet drawing. I checked with the coach to find our first assignment—and guess what it was? The rings. All that I could think about was Japan. "Great," I said under my breath, "that's all I need. I get to start on those stupid rings." I took off my warm-ups. Usually the first event of the competition is the most exhilarating—you really snap through your moves. If you go into a *handstand*, you are "locked." Even if somebody ran out there and shoved you, you'd still stay up. I pulled up into a *handstand* and I really had to "work" it. It was hard. Here I was in the best shape of my life and I could hardly press up into a *handstand*. This was not a good omen. But at the end of the routine I had a 9.8. I still wasn't excited. I told myself "Come on, Conner, this is the big time here. You don't have time to worry about this garbage."

Vaulting was next and I was first in the lineup. Personally, I would have loved to have been the last in every lineup. But, after all, I was the last guy to have qualified for the team—and by the "skin of my teeth" at that. Few people were counting on me to do real well. But somehow, I did the best vault of my life and got a 9.8. Still, I didn't feel right. I felt all bundled up, as if I were wearing layers of sweaters and a snowsuit.

We moved to the parallel bars and I was third in the lineup. And then something snapped. In an instant I felt like myself again. I finally broke a sweat and I moved like I wanted to. My score was 9.9.

I thought that my sluggishness must have been something phys-ical—like a buildup of lactic acid. That can slow an athlete down unless he works it out of the muscle tissue. But since the Olym-pics, I've had physical therapists tell me that I was probably in shock. The events of the previous year and the emotional release of being there were too big a jolt for my nervous system. All I can say is, thank God for *automatic pilot.*

We moved to the next event, the high bar. That's when we got the news. Jim Mikus, our alternate, had been keeping statistics. The Chinese had already finished their first round of compulsory exercises, and word came from Jim that at this point, we were seven tenths of a point *ahead* of the Chinese! You should have seen the faces of the guys on the team! Instantly we all realized that we had a shot. Instantly there were no more individual stars—we were a team. Time to get down to really thinking about what the *team* had to do to win.

Our hardest team effort was in trying to bring up each of our weakest areas. If, for example, you knew that one guy hadn't spot-ted a flaw in the way he was doing something—and if this was an event in which you were usually better—then you'd try to give him a little advice. Or watch and give him your opinion. Before the compulsories, we knew that if our lowest scores were in the 9.7–9.8 area, then we would have a shot at a medal. In all hon-esty, most of us thought that medal would be a silver, behind China and ahead of Japan. Now that could change. Especially if we got into first place on this first day. That's because there is an order to Olympic events and we could use the order to our advantage.

In the finals the top four teams would be competing at the same time. That's where all the action would be. If we pulled ahead now, we would be going head-to-head in round two with the best in the world. Competing with the best *always* brings out your best.

Second, the first-place team always goes up first in the actual lineup of events. In each phase of gymnastic competition the events follow the same order: floor exercise, pommel horse, rings, vault, parallel bars, and high bar. The first-place team starts on floor, the second-place team starts on pommel horse, and so on all around the gym.

Starting in the optional floor exercise is an incredible advantage. There are two reasons for this. First, you are in familiar territory. In many smaller meets everybody starts with the floor exercise. So, starting here is more comfortable—it seems to be the natural order of things. Second, floor exercise requires the most energy. You have to explode through it. At the end of a meet you're pretty whipped. The last thing you want to do then is to run down the mat and turn *double somersaults!* Starting with the floor exercise means that the rest of the meet is downhill. Think about the guys who had to start the Olympics on the pommel horse or the vault and you can see my point even more clearly. At the beginning of a big meet like the Olympics, you are so "juiced"—so full of energy—that you can just vault yourself to kingdom come. So in addition to starting on the floor, being in first place assures you of one last advantage: you don't have to start on the horse!

And so we entered the second day of team competition in first place, ahead of both the Chinese and the Japanese. Nobody thought we would have been in this position. Our first event was the floor exercise, and because I had scored a 9.95 in the compulsories, I had a good shot of going into the Individual finals. So this time I was last in the lineup. Tim was first up. His routine was a little shaky and he scored 9.5. Mitch was up next. He almost went out of bounds (he hardly ever does that!), and scored a 9.75. Then Jim got a 9.8, Scott got a 9.7, and Peter got a 9.8. All in all, these were low scores for our optional performances. We looked wobbly, shaky, and scared. I did my floor routine and it was one of the best I've ever been able to pull off in a meet, a 9.9. That score seemed to fire us up a little. Meanwhile, we could see the Chinese just one event ahead of us in the gym. They were doing great! Sailing around the pommel horse, racking up fantastic scores. They were catching us. Every time they would perform, the guys on our team would look to their scores.

Horse was next for us, and the Chinese were performing right next to us on the rings. We couldn't help noticing that they were awesome: 9.8, 9.9, 9.9, 9.95, 10, and a second 10! We were just about wiped out as we looked at those ring scores and then tried to do the most shaky event, the pommel horse. Our scores showed our state of mind: Peter and Tim held it together and each got a 9.9, but Mitch got a 9.85, Jim got 9.7, Scott got 9.65, and I got 9.75. Even if you know nothing about how gymnastics is scored, you can look at those sets of numbers and see that the Chinese were racking up more points—fast! I've heard some gymnasts say that they never watch the scores. I don't believe it. Some people may not watch them as much, while others may sit there with a pocket calculator, but you cannot compete like this without keeping a pretty accurate running total of the score.

Here we were all watching the scores. We were doing "okay" but the Chinese were doing "unbelievably well."

At this point the team started to get rattled. Most of the guys who were running around, talking about the Chinese scores, repeated the obvious fact that they were catching up. Somebody would say, "Did you see that? He got a ten—I don't believe it." Somebody else would answer, "My God, there's no way he deserved a ten!" Our general morale was evaporating.

I looked around for our coach and he was adjusting some equipment out on the floor. So I decided to really stick my neck out. I called the guys together and I said, "Look, we're losing it because we're watching *them*. Just for now, let's pretend that there's nobody else in the gym but us. If we want to watch the Chinese and Japanese, let's do it tomorrow with the videotape." Anybody else could have said it—we all knew it was true—it just had to be verbalized. We put our hands together and once again we were a team. After that, we each turned all of our energies to the meet. We began to challenge instead of to just hang on.

The rings were our next event and our scores were 9.8, 9.85, 9.9, 9.85, 9.9, and Mitch's 10. That 10 meant a lot. It was *much* more than simply .05 points higher than a 9.95. It meant that we too could get a perfect score.

It was at this point that the crowd became an incredible factor in our victory. We noticed that they were focusing all of their energies on us—we were the main event. While we performed the crowd was very quiet, but when we did something well, they would explode into chants and screams.

The final event was the high bar, and the mathematics between us and China meant that it was literally down to the wire. Remember, in each event the team is allowed to throw out its lowest score. We could only make one mistake. Scott was up first. After a very strong routine, he did a terrific *triple flyaway* for his dismount. But when he landed, he put his hands down. His score was 9.5. That was our one mistake. We couldn't have another one. We were scared—but we pulled it together. Jim got a 9.8, Mitch got a 9.95, daring to perform the *Gaylord II* release move for the first time in international competition, I got a 9.9, and Tim hit a perfect routine using two release moves and scored a 10.0! Peter was the last man up. It was all up to Peter now. Tong Fei was the last Chinese competitor. Our little calculators had been working overtime and so we knew at that point that if Peter could make it through a decent routine—if he didn't wipe out—Tong Fei would have to score almost an 11 in order to beat us. Peter went up and scored a 9.95. Scott, our assistant coach, Makoto Sakamoto, and I all reached Peter at the same time—we grabbed him so hard, we almost knocked him over.

Suddenly it was over. We had done it.

In the last four events we had scored several 9.9s, a couple of 9.95s, and three 10.0s! I had scored my second 10 ever on the parallel bars. But the final statistics show that we actually beat the Chinese in the "lower end" of our lineup. Our lowest scores were higher than their lowest scores, thanks to Scott Johnson and Jim Hartung, our lead-off performers.

Ten months before the Olympics, at the World Championships in Budapest, the Chinese had beaten the Russians. And it had been a long time since *anybody* had beaten the Russians. So the members of the Chinese team knew full well what it was like to come from behind and knock off the "big guys." They knew how we felt, and they had sincere joy for us in our victory. They had done their best; we had done our best and we just had a few more points. That's all. In a sport like wrestling or football, you can do something *to* your opponent and you can "take him out." It's not like that in gymnastics. You can't loosen the p-bars or spit on the mat. You aren't doing anything *to* an opponent, you're just doing the best that you can with your own body. Do your best, and if anybody beats you, then he was a better man. I look at someone like Li Ning and I feel a great deal of respect. And I feel that he has the same respect for me. After we won the team competition, the entire Chinese team came over to congratulate us. Li Ning shook my hand and gave me a look that said, "You're all right, Conner. I know that we're pretty awesome and today you guys beat us."

We put on our warm-ups and ran back to a corridor under the stands where we were to receive instructions for the awards ceremony. Everybody was slapping us on the back and giving us the "high five." We lined up in pairs and followed the volunteer guide back into the arena.

The screams from the crowd became an auditory blur—constant and indistinguishable. I felt the muscles in my legs twitch as we walked to the center of the floor and climbed onto the long, narrow platform.

I was thrilled and excited to be a part of one of the greatest team efforts in gymnastics history. I remember the contrasting emotions. I was in the center of this event, but I felt strangely distant, as if I were watching a play or a movie. So often we say that something is "unreal"—part of a dream. This was it exactly.

I looked to my right and saw that Peter was having difficulty breathing. He's always in such control—the cool and stable one—but the tension had finally exploded inside of him as he began to hyperventilate. All I could think was, *Please, God, don't let Peter pass out.*

"Take a breath. Slow down. Take a breath. Slow down," I kept repeating to him as the screams from the crowd grew more intense.

The officials came toward us with our medals. When the gold was around my neck, I looked into the face of Yuri Titov, one of the few Russians to have come to L.A. He was the President of the International Gymnastics Federation and he had been allowed to fulfill his responsibility and his honor of presenting the gymnastics medals. He smiled and slowly nodded. He knew. Now he was not a rival but a fellow sportsman.

The crowd became instantly silent and I could see the crossbar lifting up the flags. The national anthem began and my neck tightened. I mouthed the words, but no sound came out. As I wiped tears from my face I told myself, "Hold it together, Conner." But there was no way.

During the anthem Peter had his back to me, but when he turned, I saw that he had tears in his eyes too.

We had done it. We were the best in the world.

After that, it was all chaos. During the ceremony the press corps had been gathering in a room under the stands and we were whisked back to see them. Have you ever heard of a press corps giving a standing ovation? They usually don't! They usually sit down and ask questions. Not tonight. When we entered that room, two hundred reporters all jumped to their feet and cheered. Maybe someday I'll remember everything they asked and what we answered, but most of it is still just a wild blur for me. After the conference, the people from ABC television had vans and a police escort to take us to their studio for a live interview. We were all still in warm-ups, medals around our necks and wilting flowers under our arms. It's one of those crazy situations where you allow yourself to be swept away by your emotions and those of everyone else. Somebody said, "It's time to get in the van," and I just followed instructions. When we arrived at ABC, Peter said, "Can you believe that to get us through Beverly Hills the police escorts stopped three Rolls-Royces, two Ferraris, and a Porsche!"

During the press conference Jim and Scott had been pulled away from the group for the random drug check (a routine at each Olympic event). They had been taken to a clinic and filled up with Cokes and beer in an attempt to complete the urinalysis.

They were so psyched that they each downed a couple of gallons of liquid before getting out of there. And by the time we got to the TV studio, they were really wasted. As we walked onto the set to meet Donna DeVarona and Jim Lampley, Hartung said, "If they ask me any questions, you answer!"

Then we were separated for different interviews. Tim and I were put in a limousine for NBC News and taken across Los Angeles to tape a segment for the *Today* show. What a riot! This limo was great. There was a bar, a TV, and a telephone, and so we spent the trip calling anybody we could think of. It was about 1:00 A.M. when I reached some friends just to tell them that I was in the middle of the Harbor Freeway.

The crowds and the excitement continued until I found myself with the rest of the guys in the 32nd St. Cafe, a bar across from the Olympic Village. It was almost 2:00 A.M. Most of the people there had seen the competition and they were going wild! Hysterical! Everyone wanted to be *the one* to buy us another beer or a bottle of champagne. But I couldn't get into it. It wasn't that I didn't appreciate their good wishes, but I didn't want to be with strangers. I wanted to be with the people who had been with me from the start of this thing. But I didn't know where any of them were. Later I learned that Coach Ziert, my parents, friends, and family had sat on a dirt mound outside Pauley Pavilion for over three hours, waiting for me to come out. They didn't know that the team had been whisked away out a back entrance. Ever the practical one, my dad finally convinced some of them to go down the road to a place called Hamburger Haven to sit it out in comfort. My mom and Ziert stayed at the vigil a little longer before giving up as well. At the bar I barricaded myself in the phone booth and tried to call my parents, but I couldn't reach them. I called Ziert and he had just made it home. We met at some greasy doughnut shop near the USC campus. It was awful, yet it was wonderful. Nobody in there knew a thing about the Olympics. It was just us and a few other night owls having coffee and doughnuts. Talking over the competition and the past year with my coach—that was my *real* celebration, because he knew more than anyone else what an important day it was for me. What a thrill to be part of the greatest team in the world.

The Coach's Side

Because he is so intense and because he is so articulate and, of course, because he's been around so long, Bart has become a spokesman for the sport. It was never planned, but when members of the media interview a group of gymnasts, the microphone almost always goes to Bart. And this brings a new kind of responsibility. He knows that when an Olympic team or a national team marches into a reception, most people are looking at what he does. And for a young man who is serious about achieving that which is expected of him, even this has become a challenge.

All of this attention began when the media noticed Bart and his rival gymnast, Kurt Thomas. The tension and the excitement between them propelled gymnastics into the public eye. Here were two very strong, very determined people with vastly different styles and vastly different sets of values, as well as an amazingly different set of abilities. Sparks were bound to fly when they went "head-to-head." Any sports endeavor consists of two harmonious but opposite elements: the physical element and the mental/emotional element. On the physical side, Kurt was by far the better gymnast. His physical skills and talents were unparalleled. Kurt could work at a fraction of his physical ability and still beat everyone in the arena—even Bart. But Bart was the stronger of the two when it came to mental and emotional stamina. And so when the pressure was on, more often than not Bart endured. Again by his sheer will to do so.

Perhaps the best way to illustrate this contrast is with the compulsory exercises. Most people know that gymnastics competition is divided into two kinds of routines: compulsory exercises displaying the techniques of the sport, and the optional or expressive maneuvers. Bart is a very skilled technician in the compulsory exercises. He has, through practice and determination, mastered the basics. Kurt, on the other hand, was never fully committed to this side of the sport and so, in my opinion, never reached his full physical potential. What he could do was explode on the optional exercises—reach extensions that simply could not be reached or whip through a seemingly impossible and electrifying combination of movements. When he was on his mark, he could not be surpassed here. Kurt's body did things that no other body seemed capable of doing. Most people are aware of his tremendous movements on the pommel horse, and even now few gymnasts can correctly execute the Thomas Flair.

Bart's freestyle strength is of a completely different character. He begins with the recognition that this is a sport evaluated through emotional judgments. And so he uses his powerful and explosive "personality" to say to the judges, "I am here to *perform* for you." I don't know what else to call it other than stage presence and charisma. This, coupled with an amazing intellectual ability to analyze movements and arrange them in a dramatic, creative manner, makes Bart the most "artistic" gymnast I've ever seen.

When Bart and Kurt *were* American gymnastics, every meet was a field of battle. Living through this turmoil was horrendous. But in the early years (1974 and 1975) they were very good friends. And why not? They respected each other's abilities; they recognized their differences. They had a mutuality of interest and goals. But as they both began to accelerate their skills, they were noticed by the media. Here were these two terrific young athletes, head-to-head in all the finals. Even physical appearance seemed to be of interest to the commentators. Almost every news article or television report would refer to the "blond one" and the "dark-haired one." It was almost as if they were a cute little matched set of toy gymnasts.

The rivalry escalated as reporters literally incited remarks that neither Bart nor Kurt had intended to say. These reporters were creating an environment that sold stories and, frankly, one that sold gymnastics.

It became apparent that because our society is so "one" oriented, it could no longer be Kurt *and* Bart. It had to become Kurt or Bart. And that was the tragedy of the entire scene. Judges, coaches, and other competitors were asked, "Which one do you think is better?" It was inevitable that the friendship would fall by the wayside.

I think this illustrates something very destructive about our society. Here were two young men, competitors and friends, who were put under the microscope, pulled apart, and thrown back at one another. Naturally, there was a period of hostility. There were people who loved it—and profited from it. After all, sports rivalries sell tickets and newspapers.

It was a difficult and distracting period, but we came through it with no real animosity. We always believed that the entire situation would blow over, and it did. Life has a way of coming full circle. Each of these young men has matured and each has developed talents in other directions. Kurt went on to become a commentator for the ABC television network. Bart continued in competitions and began work with the NBC network. And once again their commonalities far outweigh their differences. During his 1984 commentaries for ABC Sports, no one was more fair nor more accurate, in the evaluation of Bart's performances, than Kurt. He was genuinely pulling for Bart to succeed.

That old friendship had been reestablished before the Olympics, but it was probably crystalized in a moment after our team stepped off the awards platform. All of the old anger was gone as Bart sincerely asked, "Don't you regret that you quit? Don't you miss this?" After a pause, Kurt answered, "You know, tonight I really do." This was a difficult and personally sensitive thing for him to have admitted. It would have been so easy to have shrugged it off with "No. Not really. I'm happy with my life." I think that's what many peo-

ple would have said. But Kurt didn't. Knowing the years and
the struggle that he also devoted to this goal, I have nothing
but respect for his honesty.

I got back to the apartment a little after 3:00 A.M. In a few hours
we were all back in the gym at USC—we still had two more days
of competition. That morning I rolled out of bed at about eleven
o'clock. My body was wrecked. I had pulled my Achilles tendon
in the floor exercise and every other inch of me ached and
creaked. Then I remembered one question from the previous
night's press conference: "After the win, will you guys be able to
'stay up' for the rest of the competition?" I had answered, "No
problem, we're on a roll. We aren't going to have any trouble."

"No problem," I repeated to myself as I limped to the shower,
turned on the hot water, and sat for a few minutes in the bottom of
the stall. "No problem."

The next day was Thursday and the third day of the competition. I was to compete in the Individual All-Around Finals. We
had already shocked the world by beating the Japanese and the
Chinese in team competition. We had already achieved more than
probably anyone ever dreamed possible. Now it was time to go out
there and have some fun.

Koji Gushiken of Japan took the gold medal, Peter the silver, and
Li Ning of China the bronze. Tong Fei of China was fourth. Mitch
was fifth and I was sixth in the competition. The top six scores were
separated by thirty-five one hundredths of a single point.

Going into Saturday's Individual Apparatus Competition, I was
in two finals: floor exercise and parallel bars. Everybody on the
team was still "on a cruise"—having a great time. I had been having some particularly good results with my floor exercise. Scores
of 9.9 and 9.95 had put me in a tie for first place going into these
finals and my confidence was high. Li Ning of China was on before me. He got a 10. That was no problem; I was a team gold
medalist. I walked around the mat and waved to the crowd as they
yelled and chanted, "U.S.A.! U.S.A.!" My Achilles was still hurt-

ing, but even that seemed minor when I felt that crowd. This routine was going to be a breeze. Or so I thought.

I mentioned earlier about "air sense," the ability to maintain your orientation while tumbling. Air sense does not come easily for me. I tend to be a little "chicken" on the big acrobatics moves. When I concentrate, I can do them. But when I relax too much in a routine, I'm afraid of them. I watch the other guys do a *triple back*, and they seem to just go up there and "pop" it. I need a little more coaxing and a little more mental control. I've wondered if maybe it goes back to that time when I landed on my head in the middle of my parents' living room, but regardless of how it got started, the tiniest hesitation or break in my concentration can cause me real problems in tumbling.

On the first tumbling pass I did a *full twisting double back* and I took a step, a one-tenth deduction—my score was then 9.9, tops. On the second run I took another step. Now the score could be no more than 9.8. The crowd started making low rumbles, as if they were saying, "Let's dump this guy, he's out of medal contention." I had taken my routine for granted and I had lost concentration. My final score was 9.75—fifth place. No medal.

After the competition, I motioned to Ziert to meet me outside the arena. I was a little shaken. I had been having such a magical time—everything was going my way—and then suddenly it turned around against me. It wasn't that my floor routine had been disastrous, it just wasn't good enough. And at that moment I couldn't figure out what had gone wrong.

B art entered the finals of the floor exercises in a tie for first place with Li Ning of China. He went out on the mat and his routine was shaky. After the routine, he motioned for me to meet him. He walked out of the arena, I ran out of the stands, and we met on the walkway behind Pauley Pavilion. "What happened?" he asked. It was very hard for me to be honest with Bart at that point. I was afraid of doing anything that would shake his confidence or set him back, but as a coach, I knew exactly what had happened. And so I said, "You know exactly what happened; you were too casual. You came out there smiling and laughing. Most of the time that's fine, you want to show that side of your personality, but this is serious. It's time for you to do the job you are capable of doing. Go back in there, take a few minutes away from the fun and the fooling around—and get your act together. Don't be afraid to be anxious, use that nervous energy, but concentrate on your performance."

I had two hours in which to warm up before my second event, the parallel bars. It seemed like two weeks. I went back to the warm-up room, sat on a sofa, and watched the Olympics on TV. I had wasted my chance because I had just *assumed* that the routine was going to take care of itself. The TV became a blur as I spent over an hour calming myself down, refocusing and redirecting my thoughts as to how I was going to handle the parallel bars. I had come too far to throw another chance for a medal away.

I got up from the sofa and walked across a skywalk from Pauley to the Wooden Center. Here we had been given the use of a practice gym for warm-ups. When I got there, it was empty, but soon I was joined by an old friend. I've competed against Nobuyuki Kajitani of Japan for ten years. He was also preparing for his performance in the p-bars finals. The first time I had ever seen him work I was a high school student back in Chicago. Kajitani was part of a

Japanese exhibition team, and I sat in the stands of Homewood Flossmoor High School and watched with awe and respect as he moved through his routines.

We talked a little and we helped each other adjust the height of the bars, mimicked parts of each other's routine, and offered bits of advice.

The time for competition grew nearer and we were still the only two people in the gym. The talking and joking stopped. The only sounds were the creaking of the equipment and the involuntary groans as one of us hit the floor. The warm-up was now in earnest. Ironically, we only practiced our dismounts, and neither of us could "stick it" right. I must have done ten *double backs* and I couldn't stick one.

I walked back into the Pavilion, knowing that I needed to make it happen. The pre-event ritual is always the same. All the competitors salute the judges, then each one takes a "one-touch" warm-up on the equipment and then leaves the floor. During my one-touch I felt strong and snappy. I knew I was in control again, but I still couldn't stick the dismount.

The competition began. Kajitani was up two guys before my performance. He paused at the end of the bars and then exploded: *a glide reverse straddle cut, press near handstand, giant, layaway front uprise, swing handstand, Healy twirl to upper arms, back uprise straddle cut, dip swing handstand pirouette, dip swing reverse straddle cut, drop cast to upper arms, forward shoulder roll, back uprise straddle cut, dip swing handstand, giant* down to a *tucked double flyaway* off the end. He landed like a rock. I looked to the board, but I knew what it was going to say: 10! A perfect score. I said to myself, "My God. What now?" Here I was in the Olympics with a man that I considered to be my friend as well as my opponent. When we had begun the finals, Kajitani was behind me by twenty-five one thousandths of a point, and now he had scored a perfect 10. I also *had* to get a 10 to beat him. Anything less and I knew I couldn't have won. I looked to the Japanese team and I saw my friend thrilled and elated over the best routine of his life. In the next moment I had to go up there and do the very same thing. I could only hope that the preparation and the planning had meant something. But the reality was much more immediate: *Bart, you've got to do it—and you've got to do it right now.*

As I put my hands on the bars all I wanted was a medal. I knew that I was capable of executing a perfect routine and if I would only *do it*, then I had as good a shot as anyone at winning that day. I looked toward the stands and I saw Ziert. He gave me the "thumbs up" sign and I was off.

Sometimes you reach up and it's like the equipment itself is too big or too strong. It just seems to overwhelm you. Other times you feel in control, like you could literally step over the bars. This time I was in control. I was going to *make* it happen. Every trick was hard and strong and steady. I was conscious in each position of extending and making every element sharp. I came in from the side of the bars, did a *free hip handstand* on the far bar, a *one quarter pirouette* to both bars, a *back toss*, a second *back toss*, a *stutz* to a *straddle handstand*, and a full *pirouette* to my *straddle "L."* The crowd started to cheer as I glided through the *Conner spin*. By the time I had made the full turn on one bar and pressed to a *handstand*, they had gone wild. Their energy really pushed me on. *You've got it*, I told myself silently. *Just don't mess up the dismount.* I stepped over to both bars, did a *stutz*, and got ready to swing down for my *double back dismount*. It was almost over.

Even if you had no prior knowledge of gymnastics, you could have watched TV coverage of the Olympics and come away with one solid fact: the dismount was important. Every commentator verbally punctuated every dismount: "Terrific dismount!" "Nope, he moved to the left, forget it." It seemed to reach the point where the composition of the exercise was insignificant compared to a perfect dismount. The guys on the team began to joke about how we could simplify the whole process by just jumping up and doing our dismounts. No need to do all of that other stuff—just do a great dismount. And there is certainly a reason for all of the emphasis. Let's say that an athlete has just finished a perfect routine—every move, every angle, every extension is perfect. If, when he dismounts, he steps a little to one side, that's a 9.9. If he steps a little more off-balance, that's a 9.8. Your goal, then, is to land flat on your feet—dead center, like a pregnant elephant. We say that you "stick it."

I'm not always good on my dismounts. In fact, I've had to work particularly hard at the skill. For this routine my dismount was a *double backflip.* I let loose of the bars and felt in control. The actual somersault takes less than a second—tops. But this time it seemed like four and a half minutes. As I flew through the air I said to myself, "Please, God, if there is any justice in the world—I want a little *right now!*"

I hit that floor—and it worked. I mean, it really *worked!*

And as the crowd cheered, my teammates ran over to me, and my coach and my family probably jumped out of their skins, at that moment I recognized a most spectacular irony. After all those years, it just seemed to come down to whether or not my feet moved.

Scoring that 10 was an incredible thrill. Of all of the places to get a perfect score, this was it—not a regional meet in Fort Collins, but in the event finals of the Olympic Games! Sometimes you scoot through a routine and sometimes you really nail it. I was in such a daze, I thought I had nailed the landing perfectly. Now, when I review the videotape, I see that my feet skidded backward ever so slightly, but thankfully not enough for a deduction.

How did it happen for me just at the right time? Why did I stick it and why did other gymnasts have problems? Why, for instance, did Gaylord complete a perfect routine and then take a hop in his dismount? Mitch could also have had a 10. But he didn't. Was it because he's not as good a gymnast? No way. In practice, Mitch seemed to always stick his dismounts better than any of us on the team. I could have done the same hop. Many times I *have* done the same hop. I just didn't do it on the day that it really mattered.

A strange aura surrounded Bart during the Olympics. And much of it was the energy he received from the people around him. Everyone interested in sport knew his story by now. Everyone knew what he had endured to even be in these games. And they all wanted him to succeed. Bart had so much going for him, so many people who were hoping, praying, and rooting for him to win. His success seemed to be some sort of *justice*.

This kind of loyalty extends even to the relationships that judges have with the athletes. Everyone is conscious of the obvious subjective nature of gymnastic scoring procedures. We have all watched meets in which political loyalties spill over into the evaluations. What you may not realize is that this same humanism can have a positive result for an athlete. A perfect example is the rapport which developed between Scott Hamilton and the judges in the 1984 Winter Olympic Games. Hamilton had been so superb, not only in this competition, but for years before the Olympics, that he was the emotional favorite. Everyone wanted him to win. And every judge knew that he had demonstrated the athletic skill, the creativity, and the stage presence worthy of an Olympic champion. There were those who joked that all he had to do was not fall down and slide into the wall and he would win the gold.

Bart had experienced a similar position in the 1983 World Championships. He had made the finals in the floor exercise, the pommel horse, and the parallel bars. The day before the competition an Italian judge approached Bart and said, "Please do a good exercise tomorrow, because I want to give you a ten. I have watched your career with admiration. For so long, you have represented the creativity and the art that should truly define gymnastics, but you have not been adequately rewarded. You do so much for this sport, and that should be recognized."

Bart was so inspired that he did a beautiful routine. It was absolutely brilliant. But in the very last tumbling trick (a *round off, backhand spring, double back*) he took a step. This is an automatic .1 deduction. The scores came up: 9.9, 9.9, 9.9, and 10! The Italian had made his point.

I have great respect for people with this kind of audacity. Bart's movement was not subtle, everyone in the arena saw it. But the Italian judge was telling the gymnastics community, "I know that there was a slight error, but I want you to know that this guy is doing what's right." Now, this judge could have made the same point to the guys back at the hotel bar, but instead, he decided to boldly declare his position to the world.

It happened again in the Olympics. Bart *did* move his feet a little bit on his dismount from the parallel bars. I saw it and I later heard it discussed by one of the judges. This judge felt that there was movement on the dismount, but because it was so slight, he determined that it would warrant at most a .05 deduction. However, the rules are such that he could only deduct .1. Therefore he could have only given a 9.9 or a 10. A score of 9.95 was impossible. He concluded, "I looked at my scorecard and saw no other deductions. I had a choice to make. And since it was the best routine on the parallel bars that day, I obviously elected to give the ten."

Actually, there is no such thing as a perfect 10. Any competent judge or coach can look at the videotapes of any 10 performance and find numerous ever so slight flaws and errors. These kids are not machines. The score of 10 is a composite of many factors: past performances and present expectations about the gymnast himself, the relative performances of other competitors, the position in the competitive lineup (10s rarely occur in the first or second routine—where would the judges go if someone else did better?), and, yes, even occasionally a nationalistic or political prejudice that has nothing to do with sport. I define a 10 in this way: I am sitting in my chair at an event. The routine unfolds and as it does so, I begin to sit up a little on the edge of my seat. I get completely involved with the emotion and the feeling of what's happening. I become the gymnast too. I am moved as if I had just experienced a great ballet or musical performance. I am better for having seen it. That's a 10. It's something much more than "he didn't move his feet when he landed."

The ceremony only lasted a few minutes, but standing up there on the platform for a second time, I had a lot to think about. I remembered 1978 when my friend Hisato Igarashi showed me his gold medal. The medal is actually very heavy—about a pound. And it's kind of lumpy, not smooth like you might expect. Both sides are heavily embossed. One side is the official Olympic seal (a woman in Greek robes sitting on a throne) and the other is a scene chosen by each host Olympic Committee. This year's committee designed a scene of an ancient crowd carrying a victor through the streets. I learned later that the '84 medals were cast by Josten's (the company that makes everybody's class ring) in my home state of Illinois and then finished in Minnesota. Each medal was made by hand and it was slow, tedious work, taking a craftsman several weeks to complete a single medal. The ribbons on the Los Angeles medals were the same fuchsia, gold, and turquoise seen in the banners throughout the city. These specific colors had been chosen because they were not present in any flag of the world.

Suddenly I was back to reality. The Olympic official who had presented the medals was backing away from the platform with that "little pillow" tucked under his arm. As he passed the judges, I saw my high school coach, John Burkel, not forty feet away from me. He was one of the judges' assistants and he had been there all along.

I could see a lot of people from that platform: my family, Paul Ziert, my teammates, and my former coaches. Even Keith Kleven was there as a trainer and a therapist for the Olympic teams. All of the people who had been so crucial to my success, all of those who had told me that they believed in me and would help me reach my goal.

Back in 1976 I had gone to the Olympic trials fresh with all kinds of titles: AAU Junior National Champion, USGF Junior and Senior Champion, and Pan-Am Games Champion. I was eighteen years old. That year, I got another unofficial title, Olympic Hopeful. What a burden. (If I hadn't made the '76 team, then I guess that I would have become an Olympic Hopeless.) I did make the team. But when they announced my name, I wasn't happy—I was just relieved of one pressure and filled with another to then succeed on a higher plane. Later I was ashamed of myself because I felt that I had wasted a chance to enjoy something that few other people would ever experience. This time it was different. This time as I looked throughout the arena I could clearly see both the value of my accomplishment and those people who had helped me get it.

I could also see the people who *hadn't* helped too. The ones who had politely avoided me during the recovery. The ones who had told my coach that he should stop my "sad and futile" effort. Francis Allen was there. He had been the coach at Nebraska when Hartung and I were collegiate rivals. When I was lying in that hospital bed in Salt Lake City, with the C.P.M. lifting my arm, I read a newspaper article in which Allen predicted who would make the '84 Olympic team. After listing every one of the top contenders and excluding me, he concluded, "Oh, yes, and Bart Conner might have an outside chance of making the team."

As I stood there I felt completely and totally relaxed. Every pressure was gone—I didn't have to be scared anymore. I didn't have to convince anyone that I could make it back. I'd won my medal and that said it all.

While the audience in Pauley Pavilion wanted Bart to win a gold medal, there was another audience that wanted it even more. These were the 7,500 people of Pauls Valley, Oklahoma. They were ardent sports fans and the adoptive parents of a gymnast from Chicago.

Five years earlier, when Jackie Conner got a phone call from the Pauls Valley Chamber of Commerce, announcing their plans to "adopt" Bart, her answer was an emphatic "No."

"He's not up for adoption," she told them.

But eventually she and her husband, Harold, flew to Oklahoma for a full-blown ceremonial adoption, complete with a judge, a parade, and the high school band. That simple act of friendship has blossomed into one of the most spectacular examples of fan/athlete loyalty that I've ever witnessed.

Since that time the people of Pauls Valley have faithfully followed the career of their favorite son. School children send him letters, businessmen discuss his international competitions at luncheons of the Rotary, and the ladies working at the Crabtree Pharmacy have sent him a greeting card *every* week for five years. (Sometimes two or three if there's lots of news to report.)

Townspeople attribute the idea to attorney Bob Rennie. Oklahoma is football country and like all football fans, Bob regularly devoured the sports section of the *Daily Oklahoman*. Once, after reading several pages detailing the latest gridiron exploits, he noticed a small, curt article. The story stated that an Oklahoma University gymnast (a transplant from Chicago) had just won a World Championship.

Rennie couldn't believe the irony. In a community that worshiped sports achievements, a World Champion was casually listed on the back page. Not only was this athlete being ignored, but he was alone in Oklahoma—all the way from Chicago. And so an idea was born: Bart and his gymnastics career were to become a community project.

On October 5, 1984, after their adopted son had "done them all proud" in Los Angeles, the people of Pauls Valley gave Bart a party. His parents and I were also invited, but the town wanted to see its hero.

Dr. Harry Millard, minister of the First Presbyterian Church, was our "tour guide and promotions manager." In just one day he skillfully maneuvered us through: a reception at the Chamber of Commerce, speeches at four area schools, lunch with the Rotary, a press conference (Oklahoma City's TV helicopters hopped the forty-five miles from their downtown stations), a parade of the homecoming floats, and a Dr Pepper at the Crabtree Pharmacy. Millard's philosophy was direct and effective: "I find that if you act like you're in charge, people generally let you *be* in charge."

At Jackson Elementary School, Bart stood before three hundred and fifty primary-level students who were seated on the floor of the gym. They were ringed by a perimeter of standing teachers and parents.

"Did you bring them with you?" a first-grader asked.

"Sure did," Bart said as he pulled two gold medals from his coat pocket.

Even the teachers leaned forward to get a better look.

"Would you like to touch an Olympic medal?" he asked. And before the answer could be heard, he said, "Coach and I will pass around the room so you can see one up close."

As Bart and I moved through the mass of children, it rippled up to accommodate us. Some of the children squeezed the medal I was holding, some moved their fingers across its surface, and some were too timid to touch it.

The children got understandably excited and the teachers moved in like battalion leaders to quiet them down. As we were leaving, several adults slipped away from the children. "Maybe I'd like to see those things too," they'd say, going straight for the gold.

(In fact, Bart has passed his medals around to so many such groups of school children that Josten's, the company that produced the medals, has already replaced his Olympic ribbons. They were literally tattered by thousands of little fingers.)

At Jefferson School and Lee Middle School, we were met by slightly more sophisticated audiences of fourth- through eighth-graders. In both schools cheerleaders led Bart into crowded auditoriums.

During one question-and-answer session Bart was asked, "When did you start gymnastics?"

"Sixteen years ago, when I was ten."

"Were you sorry when the Russians couldn't come?" another asked.

Bart began a serious and thoughtful response about the political ramifications of the boycott. A girl behind me said to her neighbor, "He's twenty-six? I thought he was a teenager!"

White Bead School is a small frame building surrounded by weeds and cattle fields. As we approached the school we saw children dart away from the front door. "He's here! He's here!" Bart walked into the gym and one hundred and twenty students stood and screamed. The principal paced before them in a plaid cotton shirt, boots, and jeans. It was several minutes before her gentle commands calmed them down. A brand-new set of parallel bars stood on the stage opposite the bleachers.

"I see those new p-bars back there," Bart said. "How many of you take gymnastics?"

Half of the school population raised their hands.

It was a wonderful, exhilarating day that ended with a parade to the corner of Paul and Chickasaw. Here in the center of town, everybody gathered to hear the Pauls Valley Panther band play the Olympic theme as Bart was presented the key to the city.

Pauls Valley is a community in which the people take pride in century-old brick streets and where high school yearbooks and tiaras for the homecoming court dominate the jeweler's storefront. The residents of this community appreci-

ate hard work and honest effort. But more importantly, they
had believed in Bart long before and long after almost anyone
else. And for that reason a part of those medals around his
neck belonged to them.

After the gymnastics competition, I took it easy. I visited with
some old friends and I went to see some of the other events. One
thing I did not do, however, was work out in the gym! I definitely
felt that I had earned a bit of a vacation.

While we were in training at UCLA all of the local talk was
about how the natives were going to "flee the city." Companies
announced the closings of office buildings, and workers' schedules were rearranged so that they wouldn't have to fight all of the
tourists and athletes. You could go anywhere in a matter of minutes. I was particularly thrilled to see all of the stars. I got to meet
Kenny Rogers, Jack Nicholson, Angie Dickinson—a whole lot of
really neat people. And it was so strange the way they kept acting
like they were thrilled to see us! I mean, here were all of the athletes straining their necks to see the stars, and here were all of the
stars coming over to us for autographs! Even as we competed we
would look into the stands and see celebrities like Cathy Lee
Crosby, Linda Evans, and John Travolta.

But probably one of the neatest experiences came about because
of one family's special interest in gymnastics. One week after we
had won our medals Diana Ross was scheduled to perform in the
Universal Amphitheater. Her agent, Jude Lyons, called our coach
and offered the team twenty-two complimentary tickets. After the
show, we went backstage to talk with Miss Ross and her children,
Rhonda, Tracee, and Chudney. This was not the first time I had
met them. Over a year earlier Jude had contacted Coach Ziert and
told him that because Rhonda was involved in gymnastics Miss
Ross was interested in becoming more involved in the sport. In
fact, after the Olympic trials, she offered to pay for a clipping ser-
vice for me. Because of her generosity I now receive copies of

every newspaper or magazine article containing my name. This time she had another surprise for us. "I'd like to do something for all the athletes," she said. And she arranged for me to be given one hundred tickets to another performance! I couldn't believe it. The next day I stood in the lobby of our U.S.A. apartment building

take long to dispense every one.

Olympic ceremonies were the ulti-
were all exhausted, both physically
of the time and the crowd were so
an around the field with gymnasts
eck, Tracee Talavera, and Michelle

s time with Tracee. We have known
by side for many years. In fact, if I
ld have picked her. She's got such a
example, when the gymnasts of the
y favorite candy was peanut M&Ms,
uge jar of them for my birthday—all
her that's very special. We had been
working and planning for this day.
lked to before going into my surgery
ne from her home in California, and
he gurney as they were wheeling me
overy, she told me that at the time of
ouraged with her progress and had
stics. But when she saw what I was
stick it out.

the other athletes and watched that
Of course, a helicopter was suspend-

from the crowd were so loud that they completely drowned out the rotary noise. Sitting in the middle of the field, the spaceship seemed to actually hover overhead. We leaned back and watched the longest fireworks display any of us had ever seen. Later, when the Olympic flame was extinguished, the full moon seemed to get brighter. It was a perfect night.

After the closing ceremonies, a friend at ABC Sports, Maria Pagano, invited me to attend the ABC wrap-party—five thousand people at a giant outdoor feast. There were three bands, tons of food, a dozen or so bars, and a lot of very tired, very happy television crew members. These were the guys who let the world in on the Olympics.

I remember getting back to the apartment at five-thirty the next morning and getting up at six-forty-five to catch the bus to the Century Plaza Hotel and the "Athletes' Breakfast," hosted by President and Mrs. Reagan. I had met President Carter when he had given "pretend medals" to members of the defunct 1980 Olympic team, but when I got to meet President Reagan, it was as a champion—one of the stars. When we first entered the hotel, we were told to put our bags down and go into a large meeting room. There the Olympic officials had set up a set of risers and all of the medal winners were asked to pose for the last "official Olympic photograph." Like the teachers in your grade school pictures, President and Mrs. Reagan stood in front of us, holding a banner that read: "1984 United States Olympic Champions." Some class!

Then it was time to meet the Reagans. The organizers of the event had provided a little roped-off area with a dark blue backdrop and special carpeting. Before going into breakfast, each athlete was to approach the area, tell a staff member his or her name, then wait to be introduced to the President, shake hands, and pose for a picture. When it was my turn, I introduced myself to Mr. Reagan.

"Hello, Mr. President. My name is Bart Conner."

I couldn't believe his response. He smiled and kind of tilted his head. "Yes, yes. I know who you are. The gymnastics team was very good and I'm especially glad to see that you stuck it out."

Unbelievable! The President of the United States actually said that he was glad that I stuck it out!

When I met Mrs. Reagan, she held my hand in both of her own and said, *"You were the one who made me cry."*

I was truly impressed. Everybody knows that President and Mrs. Reagan have to meet and pose with people all day, every day.

It surely must be tedious for them. But that morning they made every one of us feel like *we* were the most important people they had ever known.

After breakfast, most of the medal winners were taken to the airport and flown to Washington, D.C. It was almost midnight when we reached Dulles International, but the place was jammed with thousands of people carrying signs and cheering as we got off the planes. That was our first glimpse of what the *rest* of the country was feeling. There were television crews, bright lights, and kids screaming and going nuts. We knew that L.A. was fired up, but it hadn't sunk in at that point that the whole country was going wacko. (In fact, I'm still surprised when I'm reminded that the whole world had seen us. A few months after the Olympics, I was approached by a man who told me that he had watched the Olympics on Israeli TV.)

When I got into the Washington terminal, a television crew was there with a reporter and a young woman named Barbara. Barbara was wearing a jacket with my name embroidered on it and sobbing that she had followed my career for eight years and wanted to finally meet me. Later I learned that she had sent balloons and champagne to my hotel. Astonishing!

After the airport welcome, we climbed onto eight or nine buses headed for the hotel. By now it was almost one o'clock in the morning after a very long day and night. But the night was to be even longer. A few minutes after we had pulled away from the terminal, the buses stopped side-by-side. I looked out the window and saw that we were parked in the dark on a runway at the far end of the airport. A man's voice came over the loudspeaker and asked us to get off the buses. When we got out, we were told that the airport officials had received a bomb threat. There had been another bomb scare that day, in the Los Angeles airport, so no one minded the inconvenience. They brought out one of those mobile lounges, and we all climbed in and sat there on the runway for over an hour while the trained dogs went through the buses and most of our luggage. We were whipped. It was hot, we were exhausted, and we were hungry. Eventually, I remembered that somewhere along the way a girl in a crowd had handed me a bottle of warm champagne. It was still in my carry-on gym bag. I opened it up, passed it around, and it lasted about two seconds. I don't even think I got any. Finally, somebody else sent a second group of buses; we left our luggage to the security people and took off once again for the hotel.

All I could think about was a shower and a pillow. But when we got to the Washington Marriott—now at 2:30 A.M.—the street in front of the hotel was full of people holding signs and banners and chanting, "U.S.A.! U.S.A.!"

We spent the next day at the Capitol and the day after that in a ticker-tape parade down Wall Street in New York City. (Driving from LaGuardia in New York to the Plaza Hotel, people stopped in traffic and stood on their cars to shout and wave to us! When was the last time you've seen a New York driver smile?) I remember seeing old films of guys like Lindbergh having ticker-tape parades, and there we all were in the same scene. It was awesome! Not to mention hazardous! First of all, people on Wall Street no longer use ticker tape, so bags of confetti had to be shipped in from Connecticut. Then, as they ran out of confetti, people began pitching reems of that continuous computer paper out of the windows. You might have seen them fall fifteen stories as long white banners. Well, some of them didn't quite stream out. Instead they streaked to the pavement like big white phone books. (Newton was right!)

I also got to walk alongside Mayor Ed Koch. Before we started the parade, we each were asked to wear a ribbon sash displaying the name of our sport. I got mine, checked it out, and discovered that "Gymnastics" had been spelled "Gimnastics." I asked the Mayor if I should wear it that way or not, and he replied, "Don't worry. They'll know it's not your fault."

The next day we *gymnasts* (with a "y") were given an underground tour of Disney World. It had to be underground because when we went on the surface, we were mobbed. I was with Mary Lou Retton and Mitch Gaylord. We'd go down a tunnel and come up for a ride on Space Mountain, then go down another tunnel and come up in Pirates of the Caribbean.

That night, the Disney management gave us a spectacular reception, including a cocktail party, dinner, and entertainment. By this time I may have slept two or three hours in as many days. When the lights went down after the intermission, I excused myself to slip up to the room. I felt bad about leaving, but I had been talking to my hosts for about three hours and they said that they understood. When I got upstairs, all of the other athletes were in shorts and T-shirts. I had been the last one to leave.

The next stop was Dallas. We were introduced during halftime of the nationally televised Dallas vs. Pittsburgh game. We walked around the field, smiled, and waved flags. My brother Bruce called me after seeing the show on TV. He said, "Bart, I could tell that you were tired—you were still smiling, but your flag was drooping."

The Texans gave us quite a parade too. Everybody had his own jeep with an American flag and the Texas Lone Star. Later we had a party at the estate where the TV show *Dallas* is filmed, and there we were each presented with a Resistol cowboy hat.

Of course, Texas is just next door to Oklahoma, so after Dallas, I couldn't resist the chance to slip over the border and go home. My mom picked me up at the airport gate in Oklahoma City. Like a member of the secret police, she whisked me off to the car and went back inside to get my luggage. Nobody in Norman knew that I was back. When we got home, I sat up on the kitchen counter while she did my laundry and fixed me some dinner. I talked continuously—a mile a minute—telling her everything that I had said and then everything everybody else had said. I only got to stay for fourteen hours and then it was back to Caesars Palace to deliver a speech that had been scheduled before the Olympics.

In each of the cities we visited we were overwhelmed by the generosity and good feelings of the people we met. Everyone had shared that week in L.A., and the Olympic athletes had become everybody's "hometown kids." The banquets and the parties were followed by an extensive personal appearance tour. In fact, from August until November of 1984, I was only home two days.

While I was considered to be the *old man* of the Olympic team, and while I had experienced a degree of success and notoriety in the gymnastics community, I had no idea of the kind of public exposure this event would generate. All of a sudden people in shopping malls mobbed us for autographs. People pulled alongside of me on the interstate to honk and wave.

Undoubtedly, one of the most gratifying rewards of being an Olympic champion is when little kids, dressed in their gym warm-ups, ask me for my autograph. It's a pleasure for me to talk to them because I remember how important it was for me to have heroes. When I was beginning in the sport, I could hardly wait for the college gymnasts to come home on holidays and work out in the neighborhood gym. I'd go work out right along with them. Maybe one of them would help me with a trick, or give me a T-shirt from his school. A visit like that could keep me going for a year. If I can fill that role for a couple of kids now, then I consider it an honor.

And so in the next chapter, some of my young friends will help me demonstrate a series of exercises for the beginning gymnast.

CHAPTER 7

Future Champions
—Exercises for
the Beginning Gymnast

A Note to Parents:

This chapter is for *every* boy and girl—not just the one who is a future Olympian. That's because every child needs a program of regular exercise. Whether the goal is healthful well-being or competitive athletics, the exercises demonstrated here will provide foundation skills for the promotion of:

- muscle tone and flexibility
- posture and spinal flexibility
- cardiovascular stimulation
- gross motor development
- development of those neurological pathways essential for mind/body coordination

These exercises are ones you can supervise in your own home—no special gymnastic apparatus is needed. A tumbling mat would be ideal, but you may use a firm padded surface such as a bedroom carpet. (Avoid loose area rugs, as they can slip and may cause injury.)

Some parents have apprehensions when a son or daughter wants to enter a gymnastics program. Their questions seem to fall into two major categories: isolationism from other activities and physical safety. Usually these concerns have originated not from experience with a general gymnastics program, but rather from the highly publicized and unique lives of top-level competitors. For example, mothers eager for their daughters to participate in other exercise programs may associate gymnastics with the television essays on Olga Korbut and Nadia Comaneci. After seeing one such essay, any parent could imagine a child being sent to live with several other girls in a Spartan sports commune. Here ten-year-olds rise at dawn, tape bleeding fingers, and march single file into a cold gymnasium. Such an image is obviously misleading. Only a fraction of the most physically gifted individuals will ever pursue specialized training programs. And when they do, it's never as dramatic as a TV special.

Even if your child should become next decade's star, it may not be necessary for him to live away from home. In the past, American gymnasts of international caliber could only find three or four equally competitive programs. That's no longer true. The sport has expanded so much that most communities have facilities and coaches quite capable of high-level training.

Yet, for the overwhelming majority of children, gymnastics is but one single element in an all-around program of social and physical development. Let your children explore the joys of gymnastics, but always allow them the freedom to walk away from it.

As with any activity involving children, special precautions must be taken to avoid injury. If you place a couple of unsupervised four-year-olds in a padded room, one of them is likely to be injured. Supervision for any program of gymnastics is essential.

The experiences a child has in the early stages of learning a tumbling move, for example, can be very important to his future success. Obviously, there is a safety factor, but there is also a necessity to instill confidence in a child regarding his ability to respect and finally execute a maneuver that is difficult. I can illustrate how early training can have long-lasting effects upon future performance. There is a simple trick off the high bar that is called a *fly-away*. You do a *giant swing*, let go, do one flip, and land on your feet. When I was in high school, I learned this skill in one day. Immediately after that I began doing the trick with a *full twist*. I never again did the simple *fly-away*. It is a basic rule of gymnastics that everyone, at any level, should maintain those progression skills that lead to the highest level of performance. But my coach had encouraged me to forget the *fly-away* and go directly to the *full twist*. He did this because of a problem *he* had with the trick. There is a moment in the *fly-away* when you are unable to see the floor—you are, in fact, momentarily lost in mid-air. Ten years later I learned that when he was a gymnast, my coach was scared to death of this maneuver. And so, not wanting to force me to do what he disliked, he had me slide through that more basic move.

It's important that you avoid making a similar mistake with your child. If you have any apprehensions about a movement or trick in our exercise or tumbling program, carefully study the instructions and accompanying photographs. Each move requiring adult assistance has been identified and includes ways in which you can "spot" or assist your child. Learn your role in the program and your child will benefit from your confidence.

Our instructional program is intended for the beginning gymnast and can be practiced at home in preparation for gymnastics class. It stresses overall large muscle development and the mastery of primary tumbling skills. I've read many gymnastics books and most are too theoretical. Specific skills are dissected and analyzed with terms like *angular momentum* and *moment of inertia*. Our philosophy is to keep it simple. Tell a ten-year-old that you want her to "accelerate her angular momentum" and you've lost her. Rather we will say, "Lift your head and the trick will work."

Nevertheless, there are a few basic concepts about movement that can help explain the goal of each exercise. Human movement can be divided into three categories: stability, locomotion, and manipulation.

Stability is what you do every day to keep your balance. As you walk or sit you are constantly using muscles to keep yourself from falling down. That's stability in action. In gymnastics the most common stability movements are bending, rolling, stretching, and stopping.

Locomotion means action—what you do when you change position. Most gymnastics movements fall into this category and include walking, jumping, running, and turning.

Manipulation is the term used to describe motion with an object. If you use your hands or feet to move with an object such as a ball or a hoop, that's manipulation. Common examples are catching, throwing, and kicking.

The purpose of any physical education program is to teach your child to function efficiently with all three types of movement.

Beginning gymnastics can be a safe, challenging, and healthful way to translate that educational theory into fun for your child.

WARNING FOR PARENTS

Do not let your child practice the following skills unless he or she is supervised. While every movement selected is well within the range of normal physical capabilities, accidents can and do occur. Therefore, it is *essential* that an adult be present to "spot" or catch each move. Knowing that you are there to prevent any hard falls will give your child a sense of security. In this relaxed atmosphere he or she can both enjoy the exercises and gain maximum physical benefit.

The Coach's Side

The following instructional material consists of two sections: Warm-Up Exercises and At-Home Tumbling Skills.

The chapter concludes with a pictorial glossary in which Bart demonstrates some original moves that he helped introduce into gymnastics.

The first section has been developed from the stretching and warm-up exercises that Bart uses before each gymnastics workout. These exercises can help *any* individual increase muscle tone and flexibility. The warm-up is essential for any exercise program in that it minimizes the risk of muscle cramp, overstress, or injury.

In the second section Bart shows boys and girls some of the tumbling moves that are basic to every beginning gymnastics program. These moves are designed to be done at home. And it can be a great advantage for your child if he or she masters these skills before enrolling in a gymnastics class.

And finally, Bart demonstrates some of the advanced gymnastics skills that helped him earn two Olympic gold medals.

THE FOUR BASIC GYMNASTICS POSITIONS

It's important for the young gymnast to understand the four basic gymnastics positions.

These are: the Tuck, the Pike, the Straddle, and the Layout. Megan (age 3), Bart, and Shannon (age 5) demonstrate the four basic positions.

Tuck

Pike

Straddle

Layout

WARM-UP

Use the following ten stretching movements to help warm up your body before any physical exercise.

If possible, begin this program after you have jogged a few minutes. This will help get your blood circulating and make the stretching easier. If it's not possible to jog, you may still benefit from these exercises—but approach them more slowly. Begin with Exercise 1 and follow through in order.

Exercise 1: THE SQUAT POSITION

Clayton (age 5), Megan, Bart, Shannon, and Josh (age 6) demonstrate the Squat Position. The hands are placed flat on the floor and the knees are held together. Hold this position for five seconds.

Exercise 2: THE STANDING PIKE

Extend your legs from Exercise 1 position. Hands should still remain flat on the floor. Here the knees should be as straight as possible. Hold this position for five seconds.

Exercise 3: HALF SQUAT/HALF STRADDLE

Return to the squat position. Keeping your right knee bent, move your left leg straight and to the side. Keep your hands flat on the floor in front of you. Hold this position for five seconds.

Now switch position, bending your left knee and placing your right leg straight and to the side. Hold for five seconds.

Exercise 4: HURDLER'S STRETCH

Clayton, Bart, and Josh show you the Hurdler's Stretch. Sit on the floor with your left knee bent and with your left heel touching your bottom. Your right leg should be straight and as far to the right side as possible. Move both arms along your right leg until your chest touches your knee. Hold for five seconds.

Keeping your legs in the same position, sit up. Put your hands on the floor between your legs. Slide your hands straight forward as far as you can and hold for five seconds.

Keeping your legs in the same position, sit up. Now lie back. Try to keep your bent knee on the floor or as close to the floor as possible. Hold for five seconds.

Now repeat the entire exercise bending your right knee and stretching your left leg.

Exercise 5: THE SITTING PIKE

Clayton, Bart, and Josh demonstrate the Sitting Pike. Sit on the floor with your legs straight in front of you, feet together. Point your toes. Put your hands on your legs and slide them toward your ankles as far as you can. Try to put your face on your knees. Hold for five seconds. Sit up.

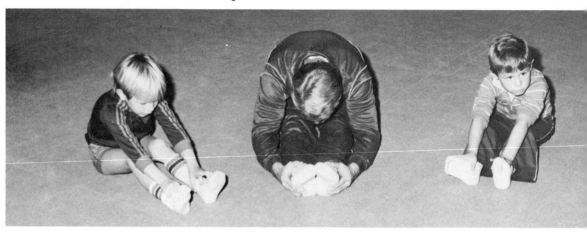

Keep your legs in the same position. Reach down and grab your toes. Gently pull your toes toward your body. Hold for five seconds.

Clayton, Bart, and Josh show you how to do the Sitting Straddle. Sit on the floor. With your legs straddled as wide as possible, put both of your hands on your right leg. Slide your hands down your leg as far as you can. Hold for five seconds. Try to keep your knees straight. Sit up.

Keeping your legs in the same straddle position, put both hands on your left leg. Now slide down this leg as far as you can. Hold for five seconds. Again, try to keep your knees straight. Sit up.

Keeping your legs in the same straddle position, put your hands on the floor in front of you. Now slide your hands straight forward as far as you can. Hold for five seconds. This part of the exercise is called a Pancake. Sit up.

Exercise 7: THE SPLIT STRETCH

Clayton, Bart, and Josh demonstrate the Split Stretch. Put your left leg forward and your right leg directly back. Put one hand on each side of your left leg. Hold for five seconds. (Don't put your hands on one side as Josh is doing.) Straighten your legs as much as possible.

Now put your right leg forward and your left leg back and repeat the exercise for five seconds.

Exercise 8: THE SEAL POSITION

Megan, Bart, and Shannon demonstrate the Seal Position.
Lie on your stomach with your hands (palms down) close to
your chest. Now, pushing up, straighten your arms, keeping your
hips as close to the floor as possible. Your head should be held
back as far as you can as you try to look to the ceiling. Hold for
five seconds.

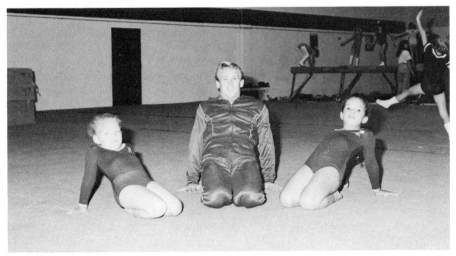

Exercise 9: THE KNEE STRETCH

Sit on your heels with your knees together. Put your hands on the
floor behind you and hold for five seconds.

Exercise 10: THE BACK BEND

Lie on your back with your knees bent as much as possible. Your hands should be on the floor (palms down) right by your ears. Your fingers should point toward your shoulders and your elbows should point to the ceiling. Now, by straightening your arms and legs, push your stomach as high as you can. Hold for five seconds. Notice that in the picture, Shannon is doing the Back Bend by herself, while Bart helps Megan.

BASIC TUMBLING SKILLS

Skill 1: THE FORWARD ROLL

Bart helps Shannon learn a Forward Roll.

2) Squat down, placing your hands on the floor in front of you.

3) Put your chin on your chest and lower the back of your head to the floor between your hands. Push yourself forward by straightening your legs.

1) Stand up straight with your hands stretched toward the ceiling.

(more)

4) After you have straightened your legs, you should have rolled onto your back.

5) Continue rolling to a sitting position with your knees bent and your feet on the floor.

6) Now stand up, finishing the Forward Roll in the same position in which you began.

Skill 2: THE BACKWARD ROLL

Nathan (age 8) does a Backward Roll with Bart helping. This is a skill that an adult _must_ help you learn.

1) Stand up straight with your hands stretching toward the ceiling.

2) Squat down, placing your hands on the floor next to your hips.

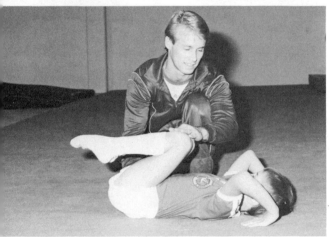

3) Roll onto your back, keeping your knees bent. Before you roll onto your shoulders, place your hands (palms down) close to your ears with your fingers pointing toward your shoulders.

(more)

PARENTS: This is the critical part of the skill. To avoid injury to the neck, it is essential that you lift your child and support his weight until his feet reach the floor.

4) As you roll from your shoulders onto the back of your head, you must push against the floor with your hands and continue to keep your knees bent.

5) You should now have your feet on the floor, knees bent, and hands on the floor in front of you.

6) Stand up with your hands over your head, returning to the position in which you began.

Skill 3: THE CARTWHEEL

CAUTION: Be sure that you perform this skill in a large open space.

Clayton does the Cartwheel with Bart's help.

NOTE: Here the gymnast may perform a Cartwheel to the right or left. In our illustration Clayton is performing a Cartwheel to the right. The adult helping you should be behind you. The entire skill should be performed on an imaginary straight line.

1) With your arms pointing to the ceiling, kick your right leg up and place it in front of you.

2) Lean forward and place your right hand on the floor in front of your right foot. Your left arm should be reaching toward the ceiling.

(more)

3) Kick your left leg and straighten your right leg. At the same time, place your left hand on the floor on that imaginary straight line. At this moment you should be on your hands with your feet in the air (legs straddled).

PARENTS: Help your child rotate through the Cartwheel and keep him on the imaginary line by supporting his waist. Be careful not to lean forward or you will be kicked in the head.

4) Put your left foot on the floor and start to stand up.

PARENTS: You still may need to support your child.

5) Finish the Cartwheel standing straight up with your hands over your head.

Skill 4: THE HEADSTAND

Shannon does a Headstand with Bart's help.

Squat down. Put your hands on the floor (palms down) by your knees. Your fingers should be pointing forward. Put the top of your head on the floor in front of your hands. Your head and two hands should now form a triangle.

With an adult's help, straighten your legs and point your toes toward the ceiling.

You should now be in a perfect Headstand like Shannon.

PARENTS: Notice that Bart is holding Shannon's legs to help her balance.

Skill 5: THE HANDSTAND

Nathan does the Handstand with Bart's help.

PARENTS: This is a very difficult skill and therefore assistance from an adult is essential.

1) Stand up straight with your arms stretched toward the ceiling.

2) Step forward with either leg. Nathan uses his right leg.

3) Place your hands on the floor in front of you. Kick your back leg up as you straighten your front leg. Notice that Bart is holding Nathan's legs to help him balance. Be sure to keep your arms straight.

PARENTS: Be careful or you will be kicked in the face.

4) Bring your feet together over your head, pointing your toes toward the ceiling.

5) You should now be in the Handstand position, and with an adult's help you should be able to hold it without moving your hands.

Skill 6: THE FRONT LIMBER

Adam (age 7) does a Front Limber with Bart spotting. This is the most difficult of our skill series.

1) Stand up straight with your arms stretched toward the ceiling.
2) Step forward with either foot. (Adam is using his left foot.)

3) With the adult assisting in the same way as for the Handstand, kick up to a Handstand. Hold this position until your spotter is prepared to help you lower your feet to the floor in a Backbend position.

PARENTS: Be sure to give lots of support to your child's lower back until his feet touch the floor.

4) Lower your feet to the floor, finishing in a Backbend position.

5) With the help of your spotter, stand up.

6) Finish the Front Limber standing up straight with your arms stretched toward the ceiling in the same position in which you began.

BART'S GYMNASTICS TRADEMARKS

In the following section I show some of those original skills that I have helped introduce into gymnastics.

THE CONNER SPIN ON PARALLEL BARS

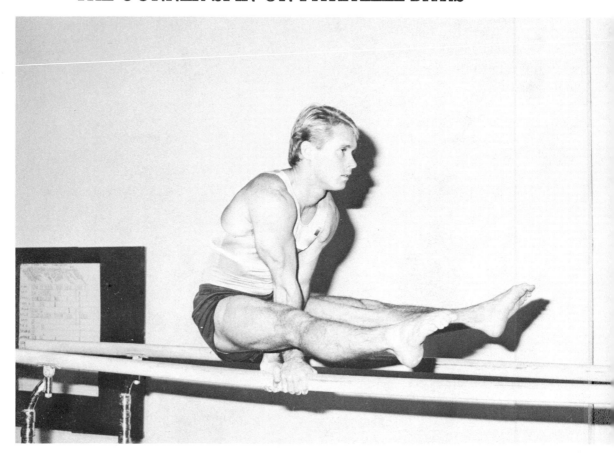

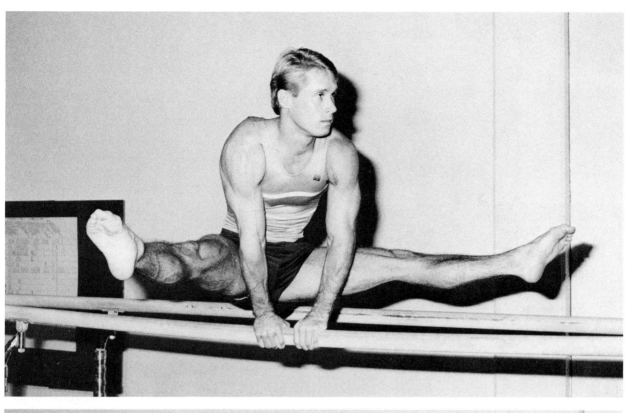

THE HANDSTAND DISMOUNT
ON POMMEL HORSE

THE "V" SEAT, PRESS TO PLANCHE, PRESS TO HANDSTAND ON FLOOR EXERCISE

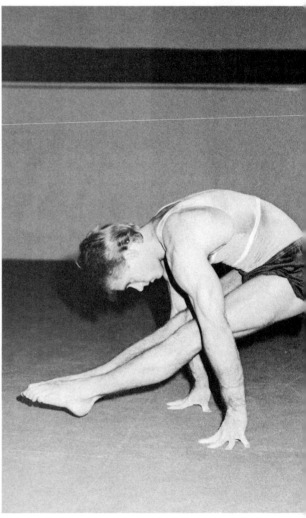

One of the things that I enjoy doing now is coaching kids. Here I show Kenny (age 7) a part of the Conner Spin.

The Coach's Side

Being Bart Conner's coach has certainly been the challenge of my life. It sounds trite, but it's true. He is a complex bundle of contradictions: his body should not be able to perform what it does—but it does. He should have been beaten by injury and failure—but he wasn't. I don't know how it comes together. I honestly don't! I'm just grateful to have been a part of it.

So far I've been able to keep my balance. I understand that some of the attention is temporary. The medals, however, are forever. They represent an experience that can never be taken away from me or my teammates. Still, they too will eventually become a part of the past. When I'm ninety years old, I'm not gonna walk around "the home" with two gold medals hanging off my neck. I have lots of other things to accomplish. Lots of other goals.

BART CONNER

1972 AAU Junior National Champion

1974 USGF Junior National Champion

1975 USGF Co-Champion of the USA:
Senior Division, All-Around

1975 Pan-American Champion: Team

1976 U.S. Men's Olympic Gymnastics Team:
Youngest Team Member

1976 American Cup Winner

1978 NCAA Champion: All-Around

1979 Champion of the USA:
Senior Division, All-Around

1979 World Cup Champion: Pommel Horse
First and Only American to Win at World Cup

1979 World Champion: Parallel Bars

1980 U.S. Men's Olympic Gymnastic Team:
Highest Qualifier

1981 American Cup Winner

1982 American Cup Winner

1984 Olympic Champion:
Team and Parallel Bars

Three-Time Olympic Team Member: 1976, 1980, 1984

Fourteen-Time NCAA All-American

Thirteen-Time Finalist at World Championship (U.S. Record)
Three-Time Winner of the American Cup: 1976, 1981, 1982 (U.S. Record)

The *Only* American Gymnast (Male or Female) to Have Won Gold Medals at Every Level of Gymnastics Competition, National and International